An Advent Journey
Through the Lineage of Christ

RIKI YARBROUGH

The Branch of a Christmas Tree

010518

Cover artwork and design by Riki Yarbrough
Edited by Heidi Burns

All emphases in Scripture quotations have been added by the author.

ISBN-13: 978-0-9996981-0-5

To my husband, Jeremy,
and my children, Micah, Payton, and Grayson:

You are the family tree He has given me
and I couldn't be more grateful.

CONTENTS

PREFACE

I came across the Jesse Tree about a decade ago while searching online for a simple but meaningful Christmas tradition our family could adopt. It was the iconic images that first caught my attention. Ornaments were to be decorated with recognizable symbols and pictures to adorn "Jesse's tree" in order to retell the story of Jesus' first coming. Each evening, a new ornament would be discovered, explained, and hung in anticipation of the day we would celebrate the Messiah's birth. I was convinced I could do this, even with toddlers wrapped around my legs and a baby on the way.

That year I cut out pictures to be used as ornaments and selected verses that would describe little snippets into the lives of Abraham and Isaac, David and Solomon, Joseph and Mary. I had imagined our days ending with fire crackling in our wood-burning stove, sitting around an ornament with a symbol of Noah's ark, listening quietly to a Bible verse being read. We made an attempt that year, but in all honesty I considered it a tradition *fail.* Kids were too young. I was too tired. Most nights we tossed toys into the corner, set dirty dishes in the sink, turned off the lights on our Christmas tree, and headed to bed.

Later the following year, I was researching church history—*because who can get enough?*—and I came across a sermon series on the genealogies of Christ. Verse by verse, the pastor walked through each person named in the Messianic line. I was overwhelmed by the revelation of God's sovereignty and grace in some of the most over-looked passages in Scripture. It became the catalyst for further investigation of this royal and prophetic family tree. I followed each name to where their stories were unfolded within Scripture. Some were obscure. Others were adequately detailed and chronicled in numerous places.

As I read through Isaiah 10, where the Creator God determines to cut down His people who had become a lofty terebinth, I was struck by God's severity. But then I read on to the next chapter: "Then a shoot will spring from the stem of Jesse, and a branch from his roots will bear fruit" (Isaiah 11:1). With teary eyes I exclaimed, "There You are." It was at this point where both the genealogies and the Jesse Tree came together in my mind. I wasn't sure if it was consistent with the tradition, but I planned to make a personal study of Christ's first coming (His advent) through His recorded lineage, then utilize pictures to narrate *His* story in the days leading up to Christmas.

For nearly eight years now, this is how our family has anticipated Christmas Day. For each individual or period of time in the lineage of the Messiah, I designed iconic images and placed on round wooden magnets. We call them "seeds". In the last week of November, we set out an aluminum-backed canvas with a painted tree silhouette. Each evening, my husband and I hide one of the seeds and allow our children to search for it. Once found, the seed is placed on the tree and we tell each other the story of what that symbol represents in the line of Christ. Some evenings we'll read the narrative I wrote including illustrations they quickly recognize. At other times, we read the story directly from the Bible. But my favorite moments are when we tell the story to each other from memory, each person breaking in to share a significant part.

The contents of this advent journey are the result of a *personal* study to uncover and understand why the lineage of the Messiah is recorded in Scripture. I did not purpose to write a family advent devotional, but it *did* serve as a resource for those evening family discussions, even for my little ones during that season. We've never skipped over the difficult ones, even Judah's heartbreaking turn. If it was not skipped in the Biblical genealogy then we believed the inclusion was purposeful. However, we did adapt details of all the stories to be age appropriate. One of the greatest benefits of slowing for advent is to be reminded that God superintends all things, including the tainted pieces, to bring about His good and perfect will.

At a later date, I chose to develop experiential prompts for each day's focus. I wanted to employ imagery and experience to aid in bridging knowledge to application and facts to obedience. These were designed as supplemental activities to be utilized if we needed to pause and further reflect on the revelation of God in His story that day. Perhaps, these will be a resource for you as you piece together the story of The Branch. It may provide a way to bridge truth to personal response among your family, at a social gathering, or within a teaching opportunity you have during the advent season.

More than any other reason, my purpose for writing this book was to invite you to come along the sojourn with me. It's one I take every year. Putting all those names together within the framework of Scripture—the names of *people who beget other people* in this holy line—I see it all pointing to Him. No name is spoiled; no era wasted. I am convinced all over again how He is both the root and the star of this magnificent and humble Christmas tree. May you be captivated as you follow *The Branch.*

Enjoy the journey.

ACKNOWLEDGEMENTS

Every page of my Bible is revealing the One I love. Even in a list of family names, I find my God there. He is so fascinating and beautiful. The words in this book come from that on-going pursuit. I am so thankful He grips my hand, even when I don't see it.

To Heidi Burns, whose rich friendship has scoffed at the miles between us. Thank you for taking vulnerable words and helping me be a better communicator. I learn so much from your expertise and envy your bold clarity. You are a gift.

To my parents, Rick and Pat Perkins, whose mix of character I bear. Mom, you are the master of detail when it comes to text, catching things I never see. (Still picking up after me.) Your gifts provide the unseen foundation for more than you realize. Dad, it's your fault I can't stop studying. Thank you for demonstrating what it looks like to *take up your mat* and follow Him. That smile you get when you know God is good, I find myself doing that too.

Jeremy, you know the background to every piece. You've seen me cry over it and become shamelessly giddy. You know how meaningful this journey is to me. Every. Single. Year. I love that you are with me in the sojourn, forever.

Micah, Payton, and Gray, you are my joy. More than anyone, you know these stories by heart, anticipating when certain parts are about you. I love talking about you, because our family tree is God's doing too. Thank you for the ceaseless questions. Your seed-searching and hearing you retell His story - these are a few of my favorite things.

INTRODUCTION

Coming

Then a shoot will spring from the stem of Jesse,
and a branch from his roots will bear fruit.
Isaiah 11:1

Then. It is not a word you would choose to begin a story with or to end one. The term implies a pending change in a sequence or process. It's often the turning point of a story. So when I use *then* in my personal narrative, it can be a bit unnerving. It links a past I know well to an unknowable future. Those turning points are the most frightening places I've ever stood, especially when I've accepted that I can't guarantee what happens after each *then.* I'm left wondering if my life is just prey to happenstance.

David believed God had his first and final page in sight: "In Your book were all written the days that were ordained for me, when as yet there was not one of them" (Ps. 139:16 NASB). Though David admitted he lacked the power to script the *turns* in his life, he was confident he was not just wandering through his days. He acknowledged an Author, trusting that every turn, every *then*, was ultimately His and heading in a decreed direction.

Might you and I slow down this season to carefully examine a narrative sequence written in His book?

Matthew and Luke both include lists of individuals that are commonly passed over when the Gospels are read. "Perez was the father of Hezron, and Hezron the father of Ram."[1] Today, the names appear insignificant to the heart of the Christmas story, but this is the record of the ordained days lived out by chosen individuals in His story. They are God's seed growing and extending, just as He intended. And though it may seem disconnected from what we encounter today, let's open to page One, where the narrative begins. The Author alone is present with divine pen in hand. From light's first flicker in a dark expanse, a beautiful redemption story is written in holy script. Imagine God the Creator filling the pages of His book with *then* and *then* and *then*.

We may be surprised to find Genesis reveals the Creator sowing a particular seed right in the midst of the darkness. If we look closely enough, we will see Jesus. Yes, right in the beginning. And if we quiet our hearts, we will hear His name being whispered as God tends to his special planting. Just a small seed, but God knows each future branch it will bear and what each will eventually become - a Christmas tree. From the very moment He creates life out of the dirt, He zealously nurtures His seed. He gives it everything it needs. Light for its growth. Water for its thirst. Seasons for renewal. Protection for its strength.

But "a destruction is determined" (Isaiah 10:22). This well-cultivated tree will rise up against the Gardener's hand. Then the One who planted and nurtured will deliver a horrific blow, cutting it to a stump. Isaiah takes us here.

> Behold, the Lord GOD of hosts will lop the boughs with terrifying power; the great in height will be hewn down, and the lofty will be brought low. He will cut down the thickets of the forest with an

1 Matt. 1:3

> axe, and Lebanon will fall by the Majestic One. (Isa. 10:33-34 ESV)

As I wade through the tragic words of the prophet, I am cut to the quick because I've been brought low, too. I see myself despising the hand that made me. What hope is there for me? But God is not finished with this prophecy. An incredible unveiling occurs in Isaiah's graphic words. It is here God reveals a turn so significant to my very life that it pulls me into the next page of this brilliant revelation.

> "*Then* a shoot will spring from the stem of Jesse, and a branch from his roots will bear fruit." (Isa. 11:1)

There's the turn: *Hope*.

Do you want to read the full story? God has not hidden it from us. Starting at the flyleaf of this great narrative, we can follow God's *thens* to watch this Christmas tree planted, nurtured, pruned, severed, and redeemed. Together we can run our fingers along these branches, with all their gnarly turns and crooked lines, mended forks and budding growths. This tree is His planting, and by it He has taken delight in revealing Jesus Himself. We can anticipate His coming, His advent, by tracing the lineage from His first spoken word all the way to His birth.

Walking through the line of our Messiah increases our anticipation of His Coming. So during the season of Advent, let's examine the growth of this tree. Together, let's magnify the One who has superintended it all to see His Word performed.[2] May the Spirit of God illuminate the genealogies of Christ, that they would take root as rich revelations of our ineffable Messiah and His masterful redemption.

Each day of this study focuses on certain individuals listed in Matthew or Luke's genealogies, with the exception of three who are not in His physical line but significant to the context and chronology of the narrative. Additionally, three days are reserved to recognize unique seasons in the genealogy, which unveil God's sovereign work during that time. The daily study includes Scripture, background, a devotional, and experiential prompts for further reflection.

---

2 Jer. 1:12

NOVEMBER 29

In the Beginning, God

I am God, and there is no other; I am God, and there is no one like Me, declaring the end from the beginning, and from ancient times things which have not been done, saying, "My purpose will be established, and I will accomplish all My good pleasure"... truly I have spoken; truly I will bring it to pass. I have planned it, surely I will do it.
Isaiah 46:9-11

Page One of Scripture opens the curtain on the Creator God. He is the only one standing center stage. All is silent.

> In the beginning God created the heavens and the earth. The earth was formless and void, and darkness was over the surface of the deep, and the Spirit of God was moving over the surface of the waters. (Gen. 1:1-2)

In reticent darkness a voice is heard.

> Then God said, "Let there be light"; and there was light. God

> saw that the light was good; and God separated the light from the darkness. God called the light day, and the darkness He called night. And there was evening and there was morning, one day.
> (Gen. 1:3-5)

Though He has existed from all eternity, this enthralling narrative begins with just three words. *Let. There. Be.* Three words affirming intention, wisdom, and creativity.

God's words break the silence and hold our gaze to the stage. Light erupts from the deep void, causing our eyes to blink into focus. Who is this One who is calling light out of darkness, that fills the first scene of life? Even before we step foot into the Gospels, Jesus is here. This is where the revelation begins.

> In the beginning was the Word, and the Word was with God, and the Word was God. He was in the beginning with God. All things came into being through Him, and apart from Him nothing came into being that has come into being. In Him was life, and the life was the Light of men. The Light shines in the darkness, and the darkness did not comprehend it. (John 1:1-5)

Who is this "Word" that caused all things into being? John pens clearly it is none other than Jesus Christ Himself. "And the Word became flesh" (John 1:14). The uncreated Son was present in the beginning and all things were created through Him and for Him.[1] If you compare the opening verses of Genesis and John, you will uncover the Old and New Testaments knit together. In both cases, through Jesus, light emerges from darkness.

God's purpose reached further than adding ambiance when he separated light from darkness on the first day. His decree orchestrated in Genesis 1 crescendoed into the Messiah's first coming in John 1. Everything that fell in between those points in time was the revelation of the true Light of this world making Himself known and redeeming His people who walked in darkness.

---

1 Col. 1:16-17

EXPERIENCE

Take a length of rope and tie several knots throughout. Pile the knotted rope before you.

Knots can be eyesores, frustrating, and often difficult to remove. A knotted rope is imperfect and often not useable. Describe a "knot" in your life. Describe a "knot" in your family line.

Could it be that what appears as chaos actually has divine order? Do you trust that God's purposes supersede the hurt, disappointment, or fear these knots have produced in your own life? Though your circumstances may resemble a pile of knots, do you trust that He sees that rope fully stretched out, from beginning to end?

Locate the beginning and the end of the rope and stretch it out until it is straight and taut. Reread Isaiah 46:9b-11.

This is one rope, connected by the same fiber throughout. As we continue in this advent journey, we will find a surprising number of knots in Christ's lineage. We may be tempted to consider these people and circumstances as disjointed – heavenly mistakes our God had to fix. However, His Word will reveal to us a high and sovereign God whose purposes are not thwarted and whose people He came to save.

Read Psalm 16 as a prayer to the Lord.

NOVEMBER 30

Adam and Eve

[The Lord God said to the serpent,] "I will put enmity between you and the woman, and between your seed and her seed; He shall crush you on the head, and you shall bruise him on the heel."
Genesis 3:14-15

When I was a young girl, my front teeth were large and crooked, but I was none the wiser. I never perceived them as a *defect* until a cruel comment turned my smile from joy to shame. My once characteristically wide and open grin transitioned to a closed smile tightly concealing my teeth. I found myself changed, and I battled to reclaim an innocence I knew was true before. Now, every expression of happiness seemed somehow distorted. It's funny how those moments stick with you.

In the midst of Eden, we observe a similar inner shift take place. Creation was young. God had breathed life into dust and made man, then fashioned a woman from his rib. His handiwork was "very good" and by design, His creation exuded an innocence to which we cannot relate – knowing nothing but purity.

All He created was for Adam and Eve's pleasure. And among all the trees God caused to grow, He named one *the tree of the knowledge of good and evil.* Its very name exemplified God's omniscient, unlimited understanding. Adam viewed all things as belonging to the Creator, and all things he had received as a gift. What claim could he take? His existence, his very breath, was God's. Though Adam lacked knowledge of evil, man was not left lacking. All these things rightfully belonged to God.

> The Lord God commanded the man, saying, "From any tree of the garden you may eat freely; but from the tree of the knowledge of good and evil you shall not eat, for in the day that you eat from it you will surely die." (Gen. 2:16-17)

At first glance, this may seem uncharacteristic of God to place something so good before man and say he cannot take it. Our questioning uncovers our tainted view that all things within our reach must be our right. But this fruit cannot be considered a temptation unless it hooks a lust that has already taken root: a lust for supremacy. Characteristic of a foe who sought this power, the serpent entered the garden and seized this opportunity to provide an alternative option of dependence.

> The serpent said to the woman, "You surely will not die! For God knows that in the day you eat from it your eyes will be opened, and you will be like God, knowing good and evil." (Gen. 3:4-5)

Eve encountered this Tempter, yet it was her own "lust of the flesh and the lust of the eyes and the boastful pride of life" that led her to deny the goodness of God.[1] The abundantly satisfied creation doubted His sufficiency and wanted instead to have *supremacy.*

When the woman saw that the tree was good for food, and that it

1 1 John 2:16

> was a delight to the eyes, and that the tree was desirable to make one wise, she took from its fruit and ate; and she gave also to her husband with her, and he ate. (Gen. 3:6)

The woman ate. Man ate. Darkness was seen in contrast to the light, and immediately they covered themselves. In utter fear they experienced a battle unknown before. A smile was now concealed. Blessing was twisted into shame. This was the beginning of Death's prologue. Who could reverse it?

A particular blueprint was unfolded in this dark moment by the One who had declared the end from the beginning. The Judge of good and evil pulled them from their man-made covering and addressed them face-to-face. As He judged these three participants, He began to foretell The End. At the moment of complete brokenness, when Adam and Eve saw their depravity, God–full of grace–revealed the final verdict and offered a sure hope.

> [The Lord God said to the serpent,] "I will put enmity between you and the woman, and between your seed and her seed; He shall crush you on the head, and you shall bruise him on the heel." (Gen. 3:14-15)

Read the curse slowly. Only one blow is fatal. Did you hear God whisper that a promised deliverer is coming?

EXPERIENCE

Locate a scar on your body and share the story of what happened.

Did you initially cover it up? Why? Did anything change in your life after the incident took place? How did it heal? Why does the mark still remain?

Consider the similarities to Adam and Eve's response after they sinned. Their efforts to hide did not take away the sting, though they tried. The scar of sin's curse remained, serving as a reminder of their need for a Savior.

> But He was pierced through for our transgressions, He was crushed for our iniquities; the chastening for our well-being fell upon Him, and by His scourging we are healed. (Isa. 53:5)

All of creation aches for perfection, but this need will only be satisfied by One. The Great Physician will come. He will heal our wounds.

As your prayer to the Lord, read Psalm 119:9-16.

DECEMBER 1

Cain, Abel, and Enoch

So it came about in the course of time that Cain brought an offering to the Lord of the fruit of the ground. Abel, on his part also brought of the firstlings of his flock and of their fat portions. And the Lord had regard for Abel and for his offering; but for Cain and for his offering He had no regard. So Cain became very angry ... Then Cain went out from the presence of the Lord, and settled in the land of Nod, east of Eden.
Genesis 4:3-5,16

Enoch walked with God; and he was not, for God took him.
Genesis 5:24

From the Garden, sin would now be the deadly trait handed down from one generation to the next. Can you imagine how Adam and Eve felt as they relayed the story of their fall to their sons? How devastating it must have been to then identify that same prideful desire in their boys as they grew. Cain and Abel were born into sin, and now *we* relate.

When my youngest son was a toddler, we would walk to the elementary school each afternoon to meet his older siblings at the end of the school day. Most days he donned full cape and mask, seeking to deliver me from whatever danger was lurking in the next driveway. Because we were different – in pace, temperament, motivation, and ability – walking together required total engagement. I anticipated his whims, and he learned my expectations.

I remember one afternoon when he darted off like a lightning bolt, chanting some type of battle cry. I laughed and waited for him to slow, but those little legs didn't stop, and his elbows swung earnestly. I picked up my pace and snapped his name in a reprimand. But he continued to yell wildly, darting straight ahead, never once looking for danger, though cars were nearby. Finally, I caught up with him and desperately swooped that little boy up in my arms just as he stepped into an intersection. The frightened look on my face was met with sheer confusion on his.

"Why didn't you stop when I told you to?"

In complete frustration he cried, "I didn't hear you! I was yelling like a super hero!"

I wonder if Cain felt the same way, running full force ahead, confident in his course. Genesis 4:5 reveals the Lord had no regard for Cain's offering, but He was pleased with Abel's. Why? Because God preferred one's livelihood to the other? No. I dare say Cain walked in a way that seemed sufficient in his own estimation, as opposed to walking *with* God. The Scripture implies Cain *knew* he was choosing his own way. Muting God's voice with our own battle cry will never result in an earnest sacrifice.

> Then the Lord said to Cain, "Why are you angry? And why has your countenance fallen? If you do well, will not your countenance be lifted up? And if you do not do well, sin is crouching at the door; and its desire is for you, but you must master it." (Gen. 4:6-7)

The devil continues to scheme, and man continues to listen. Sin was crouching at the door, and Cain let forth his own battle cry to prove *his* way was better. Then in unrestrained revolt, he took the life of his own brother and chose to exit from God's presence altogether.[1]

Seven generations after Adam, however, one was born by the name of Enoch. By that time, the earthly population was polluted with men who followed the way of Cain, pursuing their own ways instead of God's.[2] But Enoch walked *with* God. He was yoked with Him. For 300 years Enoch walked with God. The finite with the Infinite One. He spent his days on this earth seeking God's company. Then one day God "took him" into all eternity because in direct contrast to Cain, Enoch had known God and had matched his Father's pace instead of pursuing his own.

> By faith Enoch was taken up so that he would not see death; and he was not found because God took him up; for he obtained the witness that before his being taken up he was pleasing to God. And without faith it is impossible to please Him, for he who comes to God must believe that He is and that He is a rewarder of those who seek Him. (Heb. 11:5-6)

EXPERIENCE

Take a walk with your family. What does walking together require? Consider your senses, pace, ability, even outside elements.

Walking together requires submission until one becomes so much like the other that each move is anticipated. Walking with God necessitates submission in order to progress with Him. Slowing when He slows, listening when He speaks, moving when He steps forward, heeding His guidance, remaining in His presence, not turning to our own way. Faith feeds submission because you trust His pace, His path, and His company are not just good, but altogether righteous.

What did you do while you walked together?

Read Galatians 2:20 and respond in prayer to the Lord.

---

1 Gen. 4:8-16
2 Jude 11-15

DECEMBER 2

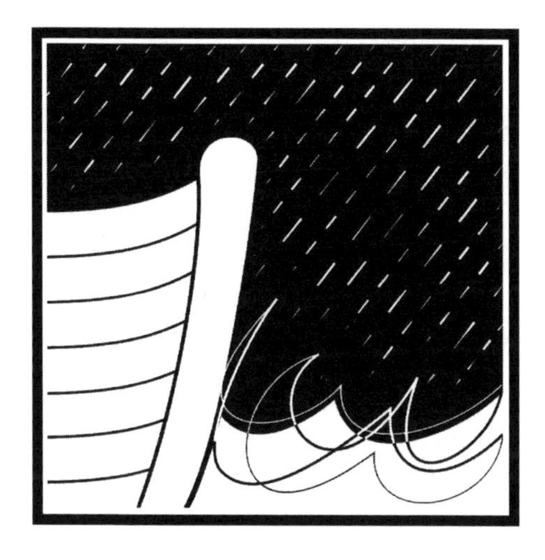

Noah

God said, "This is the sign of the covenant which I am making between Me and you and every living creature that is with you, for all successive generations; I set My bow in the cloud."
Genesis 9:12-13

For more than a 1000 years, the seed of Cain spread like a weed across the land, choking out all that was good. There was little to nourish a righteous follower of God. Even then, however, there existed a remnant.

> Noah was a righteous man, blameless in his time; Noah walked with God. (Gen. 6:9)

Noah had lived for five centuries and, much like his great-grandfather Enoch, found favor with the Lord. I would imagine by this time their *walks* were so woven into the fabric of his life, he must have wondered if he'd be "taken up," too. Instead, on one particular day, the

Lord revealed a devastating secret: "The end of all flesh has come." Then he revealed a judgment: "I am about to destroy;" a command: "Make for yourself an ark;" and a promise: "I will establish my covenant with you."[1]

Being privy to secret information doesn't always feel like a privilege. Fulfilling what God had decreed would require obedience, but that obedience would be considered ludicrous and would irreversibly alter Noah's future. Would Noah walk with God this far?

God said to Noah, "You alone I have seen to be righteous before Me in this time" (Gen. 7:1). Noah was already accustomed to trusting God in contrast to his neighbors. So when the Lord commanded him to do the most bizarre job he could have imagined, Noah surely realized the entire world would reject and ridicule him. I cannot imagine the depth of his resolve, but we find Noah choosing to take God's pace.

Twice it says in Scripture "Noah did according to all that the Lord had commanded him".[2] He didn't seek man's approval, and instead fully submitted to God's will. In his shoes, would we have attempted in some way to follow both God *and* man? Maybe search for a path with less resistance to make both happy? A partial allegiance is actually no allegiance at all.

What was God doing with mankind? It seems harsh to bring desolation to the entire earth. And yet Psalm 19:9 says, "The judgments of the Lord are true" and "righteous altogether." We tend to question the righteousness of an act when it brings destruction.

At a later time there would be another prophet who would experience desolating judgment and calamity around him. Unlike Noah, Jeremiah would approach the Lord to question the severity of God's punishment. In reply, God would take Jeremiah's hand and lead him to a local artisan.

"Arise and go down to the potter's house, and there I will announce

---

1 Gen. 6:12-18
2 Gen. 6:22; 7:5

> My words to you." Then I (Jeremiah) went down to the potter's house, and there he was, making something on the wheel. But the vessel that he was making of clay was spoiled in the hand of the potter..." (Jer. 18:2-4)

When God tears something down, his purpose is to build up, prune, reform, and preserve. In that moment, we find it difficult to see His grace. Do not forget His desire is that all would repent, and He is patient with us.[3] The destruction of the clay is a purifying means to a restored end. Even at the potter's house, God made this clear.

> The vessel that he was making of clay was spoiled in the hand of the potter; so he remade it into another vessel, as it pleased the potter to make. Then the word of the Lord came to me saying, "Can I not, O house of Israel, deal with you as this potter does?" declares the Lord. "Behold, like the clay in the potter's hand, so are you in My hand, O house of Israel." (Jer. 18:4-6)

Just as the potter did not throw away the marred clay, God does not abandon His creation. On the contrary, God is restoring man as the potter remakes the vessel he has chosen to level. God does not abandon the purpose He has for His creation, and in keeping that covenant we find magnificent grace.

Believing God's secret, judgment, command and promise, Noah spent decades building an ark to the specifications of His design. And with the sky open and the earth dry, Noah entered the boat with his family, just as God commanded. And the One who keeps His word brought the animals and closed the door.

After almost a year inside the ark, Noah reopened the door. Water had covered and destroyed everything outside those gopher wood walls. The world was silent, but his family was spared. I imagine their hearts were quiet too for they had seen God perform an awful and amazing work, born of judgment and filled with grace. He was faithful to His word. In response, Noah built an altar. His family waited to know what

---

3 2 Pet. 3:9

to do next. Then God spoke. He comforted them with His promise to never flood the earth again. He sealed his promise with a sign in the sky for every coming generation to see, including you and me.[4]

> By faith Noah, being warned by God about things not yet seen, in reverence prepared an ark for the salvation of his household, by which he condemned the world, and became an heir of the righteousness which is according to faith. (Heb. 11:7)

EXPERIENCE

When we make a binding promise, we often designate some type of object or symbol to signify that pledge. What examples can you give?

Why do we create symbols of promise? Why would God?

Have you ever unexpectedly seen one of these symbols and been reminded of a promise you or God made? Did it significantly change your perspective?

Read Jeremiah 18:1-12 and Romans 11:33-36.

4 Gen. 8:18-9:17

DECEMBER 3

Abraham

And He took him (Abram) outside and said, "Now look toward the heavens, and count the stars, if you are able to count them." And He said to him, "So shall your descendants be." Then he believed in the Lord; and He reckoned it to him as righteousness.
Genesis 15:5-6

God commanded Noah and his family to repopulate the earth, and they did. A family flourished into nations, but floundered as they separated, and eventually failed in their loyalty to God. Ten generations after Noah, Abram was born into a society that had forgotten God's promises and had turned to other gods. But God did not forget His promises. Soon after Abram's father died, God spoke directly to Abram.

> Go forth from your country, and from your relatives and from your father's house, to the land which I will show you. (Gen. 12:1)

If we contrast this encounter with God to the others we've witnessed so far within this lineage, Abram is not described as "walking with God" or "righteous during this time." Instead we find he came from a society of pagan worshipers.[1] Yet, God calls him. He calls Abram *out.* This unanticipated branch of the Christmas tree was one hidden in the back. Miraculously, it would be through *this* particular man that God would extend His covenant to and through.

At this point in Abram's story, he knows nothing more than a direction. God has not provided a destination point to where he must travel, but only a guide: "to the land which I will show you." For Abram to pack up his bags meant he trusted the Guide more than his own reason. And it was only the beginning of a sojourn riveted with trials and errors that would steadily lead to unparalleled faith in the One True God.

At one particular pause in this early sojourn, Abram's nephew Lot was taken captive as Sodom was plundered. When Abram learned the news, he took 318 of his trained men and attacked the enemy at night, rescuing Lot and bringing back the plunder. You can almost feel the adrenaline as he responded with decisive action, fueled by God's protection and promise. As would be expected, the news of Abram's success spread, and he became feared by the leaders in the area. You can almost imagine Abram completely dumbfounded for the unprecedented strength God had provided, yet utterly exhausted wondering if he would ever have to do that again.[2]

The intensity of trials can certainly leave us humbled with our strength depleted. It may have produced endurance and faith, but sometimes we come out of those circumstances with a stronger desire for control because we fear walking through that fiery ordeal again. It appears this was the case with Abram, but God hushed Abram's fears.

> *After these things* the word of the Lord came to Abram in a vision, saying, "Do not fear, Abram, I am a shield to you; Your reward

1 Josh. 24:2
2 Gen. 13

> shall be very great." (Gen. 15:1)

Before Abram could take another step on his journey, he needed to understand that his own efforts were not what sustained him. *God* was sustaining him. Abram's own strength was not what ensured the fulfillment of God's promises. *God* would see that through. What Abram didn't know was that the testing around the corner would be even greater, and it would require his full reliance on God.

But God graciously did not stop there. He continued to settle Abram. How God cared for Abram at that moment reminds me of time I had to settle my oldest child. My son experienced severe colic as a baby. After hours of unsuccessful attempts to soothe this screaming child, I stepped outside. The temperatures were freezing, cold enough to snatch the breath from your lungs. As the chill hit us full force, my son immediately went from a red-faced, screaming baby to a wide-eyed, hushed little boy. To keep my mind from thinking about the cold, I looked up to the sky and talked to my settled son about the stars I saw. On many nights, this was the only time I could talk to him without battling his cries. Just stepping outside changed his countenance.

So in the midst of Abram's anxiety about how God was going to carry out His promises and protect him along the way, the Lord changed the scenery.

> And [God] took [Abram] outside and said, "Now look toward the heavens, and count the stars, if you are able to count them." And He said to him, "So shall your descendants be." Then he believed in the Lord; and He reckoned it to him as righteousness." (Gen. 15:5-6)

The scene is incredible. One moment Abram was frightened. *Then* God took him outside, caused him to look up, and Abram was quieted in belief. He stood still, wide-eyed, and listened to God.

God sealed His covenant with Abram, making sure he understood that its fulfillment would not be based upon Abram's faithfulness but the sole work of God Himself. He would give Abram and his descendants the land, provide Abram and Sarah a son, nations and kings would come from him, and He would bless Abram and all his descendants forever. At this declaration we find Abram on his face before the Lord. He is a changed man with a new name: *Abraham.*[3]

It was God who compelled Abraham through each maturing step of his sojourn. Abraham could not boast, only pattern God's workmanship.[4] And to our benefit, we can witness how God's grace is truly unmerited, His strength is unmatched, and His calling is sure.

EXPERIENCE

Consider the areas you have traveled in your lifetime. Perhaps you've moved locations or taken trips to various places. Find a map that includes those areas and briefly share your life's sojourn to this point. Let your finger travel your journey and include simple descriptions of what those locations mean to you.

Were there points where you were frightened or circumstances seemed out of control? Were there places where you were tested greatly or where God shifted your perspective?

Read Isaiah 41:10 and James 1:2-4. Can you testify to these things?.

---

3 Gen. 17:1-8
4 Eph. 2:9-10

DECEMBER 4

Isaac

Now it came about after these things, that God tested Abraham, and said to him, "Abraham!" And he said, "Here I am." He said, "Take now your son, your only son, whom you love, Isaac, and go to the land of Moriah, and offer him there as a burnt offering on one of the mountains of which I will tell you."
Genesis 22:1-2

Abraham was 100 years old when his wife Sarah gave birth to Isaac. Abraham tried to work the circumstances to fulfill the promise sooner, but God proved again His promises do not rest on the workings of man, nor is He limited by our expectations or our interferences. Even when Abraham seemingly derailed God's plan by *helping* Him along, God intervened and the sovereign tapestry was still woven by His hand alone.[1] A tangled mess became a significant component as Abraham

1 Gen. 16; 17:15-21

began to trust the One who was capable to bring about exactly what He said.

This is also where the word *love* appears for the first time in Scripture. God notes Abraham's affection toward his son Isaac and instructs him to take his "only son" to another land and sacrifice him there.[2]

I pray that you are moved to worship your Sovereign Lord as you see how this request is such a marvelous foreshadowing of what God Himself will do to save His people – you and me.

Though Isaac was not the firstborn to Abraham, he was the chosen vessel to receive the promise, the blessing. Even when Abraham questioned this, God made clear that "through *Isaac* your descendants shall be named" (Gen. 17:19). Again, Abraham was tested. Up to this point, there are several accounts where Abraham took matters into his own hands, as if God needed him to forge a way of fulfilling those promises. And each time God proved He needed no assistance. So this time,

> Abraham rose early in the morning and saddled his donkey, and took two of his young men with him and Isaac his son; and he split wood for the burnt offering, and arose and went to the place of which God had told him. (Gen. 22:3)

> By faith Abraham, when he was tested, offered up Isaac, and he who had received the promises was offering up his only begotten son; it was he to whom it was said, "In Isaac your descendants shall be called." [Abraham] considered that God is able to raise people even from the dead, from which he also received [Isaac] back as a type. (Heb. 11:17-19)

Abraham could not reason how Isaac would be the father of many generations if this boy was also to be put to death as a sacrifice. But *this time* instead of looking for a loophole, he trusted God would somehow flawlessly merged these two declarations, even if He had to raise Isaac from the dead. Abraham's actions proved the depth of his faith.

---

2 Gen. 22:1-2

> Abraham took the wood of the burnt offering and laid it on Isaac his son, and he took in his hand the fire and the knife. So the two of them walked on together. Isaac spoke to Abraham his father and said, "My father!" And he said, "Here I am, my son." And he said, "Behold, the fire and the wood, but where is the lamb for the burnt offering?" Abraham said, "God will provide for Himself the lamb for the burnt offering, my son." So the two of them walked on together. Then they came to the place of which God had told him; and Abraham built the altar there and arranged the wood, and bound his son Isaac and laid him on the altar, on top of the wood. Abraham stretched out his hand and took the knife to slay his son. But the angel of the Lord called to him from heaven and said, "Abraham, Abraham!" And he said, "Here I am" He said, "Do not stretch out your hand against the lad, and do nothing to him; for now I know that you fear God, since you have not withheld your son, your only son, from Me." (Gen. 22:6-12)

Do you hear God whispering the Messiah's name again? Do you hear Him declaring the end from the beginning? In this scene God visually demonstrated how He would save us. Though our rescue seems impossible, though we see no reconciliation of judgment and grace, watch here! Watch what the Lord performed through Abraham and Isaac! Grasp His love for you and me, how He sent His Son, His only Son, who carried the wood on His back, walked up a hill, and became a sacrifice for us. It is on *that* hill where God would provide *again.* But this time the angels would be silent. No one would stop Death's hand. The Son would die. Sin would rest on *Him*, and our life would begin. Can you see it?

Therefore, God made provision for Isaac's preservation. Once Isaac grew to be a man, Abraham desired that his heir would find a wife from his own people. Abraham and his servant earnestly sought God's clear direction and found Rebekah to be the suitable partner for Isaac. Again, we see the term *love* used here, for the account says, "[Isaac] took Rebekah, and she became his wife, and he loved her" (Gen. 24:67).

Know this: God, too, will send His son to pursue His bride. And He will love her to the end.

> For God so loved the world, that He gave His only begotten Son, that whoever believes in Him shall not perish, but have eternal life. (John 3:16)

EXPERIENCE

Find an object that represents your life right now and explain what it means.

If we could have written our own stories, I imagine we might have penned them differently. Even where we stand now, we might have the desire to pluck the pen from God's hand. Yet, our view is so limited. Right now we can't see how our lot is necessary for His work. Can we trust Him with that? Can we trust He loves us when things seem impossible? Do we have the faith to leave the pen in His hands?

Read Isaiah 55:8-11.

DECEMBER 5

Jacob

"Behold, I am with you and will keep you wherever you go, and will bring you back to this land; for I will not leave you until I have done what I have promised you."
Genesis 28:15

Isaac and Rebekah were married for 20 years before the Lord removed her barrenness. She gave birth to twin boys: Esau and Jacob. Esau was the firstborn, and of course, was expected to receive the larger portion of the inheritance and blessing. This was a particularly significant position in this family because God's covenantal blessing was promised to be extended through one son. Against our expectation, God chose the younger of the two boys to be the recipient of His blessing. This surprising turn of events was fulfilled over a bowl of stew and the contrived efforts of an over-zealous mother.[1]

---

1 Gen. 25:27-34; 27:1-40

As I sit here writing this account, I have been battling distraction. The past couple of weeks have been filled with tasks and expectations that have compounded into a confusing mix of voices. And yet, if I wait and listen, I hear God turning my attention to this particular text. I need it today.

Yesterday I held the bread and cup in my hands as I joined with the rest of the congregation in communion. A magnificent duo of guitar and string bass created the backdrop of the ordinance. I worked to dedicate my thoughts to the meaning of what I held in my hands. However, my mind bounced between the disappointments of the previous week, a new overwhelming task ahead of me, and the conversation I needed to have after the service. I phased in and out of what my pastor was reading from Scripture – excerpts of the Lord's words from His final Passover meal. "Remember Me," I heard him say. "Remember Me." *Yes, yes. Remember Jesus ... and all these other things that are causing my heart to fail right now.*

Then *click. Click, click . . . click. Tap, click, tap, tap . . . tap, click.*

I looked up, and everyone sat still. The clicking and tapping increased in frequency and ferocity. Pieces of ice began pounding the metal roof of our church in its own song. Stronger and stronger the ice pounded over our heads. Its volume rose, and every eye was fixed upward. Soon everything else was washed out by the sound. We were all still. My heart became focused.

"Remember Me!" My God reverberated. A huge smile stretched across my face. I wanted to jump from my seat. Sometimes the Lord silences us with a whisper, but other times His voice drowns out all other noise.

As I reread Genesis 27, I noticed the repetition of two phrases: "behold" and "listen to me." *Behold* is similar to saying, "Look here!" And "listen to me" demands immediate attention and obedience. In all, it's mentioned over 10 times. A battle ensued within Isaac's family among the phrases within this particular scene. You can feel the tension rising. *Behold* this, *behold* that, until we reach a point when we don't know exactly what to behold or how to obey.

Jacob was caught in the midst of this battle. Eventually, he caved to the manipulation of his worried mother, Rebekah, which led to deception, pain, and a forced escape from the fury of his brother Esau. *Behold* a man fleeing from confusion and heading to a land far away from home, his spiritual compass all askew. Surely the God of his father and his father's father was far from him.

Jacob arrived at a familiar place to spend the night under the stars, the same stars his grandfather was instructed by God to count. He fell asleep with his mind racing and his heart failing. He was not fit to receive the blessing from his father. But then Jacob fell into a deep sleep and had a dream.

> *Behold,* a ladder was set on the earth with its top reaching to heaven; and *behold,* the angels of God were ascending and descending on it. And *behold,* the Lord stood above it and said, "I am the Lord, the God of your father Abraham and the God of Isaac; the land on which you lie, I will give it to you and to your descendants…in you and in your descendants shall all the families of the earth be blessed. *Behold,* I am with you and will keep you wherever you go, and will bring you back to this land; for I will not leave you until I have done what I have promised you."
> (Gen. 28:12-15)

A ladder appeared in the dream, showing access from earth to heaven. The Lord reiterated His blessing through him and promised His presence. And above all the noise in Jacob's head, he heard the voice of the Lord speaking louder, "Behold! Listen to *Me*! I am with you!" And Jacob's chaotic heart was silenced.

> Then Jacob awoke from his sleep and said, "Surely the Lord is in this place, and I did not know it." He was afraid and said, "How awesome is this place! This is none other than the house of God…" So Jacob rose early in the morning, and took the stone that he had put under his head and set it up as a pillar and poured oil on its top. He called the name of that place Bethel (*meaning The House of God*).
> (Gen. 28:16-19)

Where the Lord was least expected, least deserved, was exactly where Jacob found Him. At Bethel, God pruned this weak branch in order to establish him as the namesake of a most prominent family. Through courtship and marriage, reconciliation with his brother, and the heartbreaking *loss* of a son, Jacob would mature to understand the sustaining strength of God's faithfulness and grace.

EXPERIENCE

Allow each individual to find a rock outside, no matter the size. Have the individual with the largest rock place it on a flat surface and share about a fear or circumstance in life that has an unknown outcome. The person with the next largest rock can then stack it on top of the first rock and share. Continue one by one until the smallest rock is balanced on top.

Do you trust God's promises and His presence as you deal with each of these fears and circumstances?

Remember: Do not be afraid, for surely God is in this place. He provides truth and His gracious love in the most surprising places.

Read Psalm 23; 138:7-8 and 139:7-12.

DECEMBER 6

Joseph, the Son of Jacob

Now, therefore, it was not you who sent me here, but God."
Genesis 45:8

Parents hope to guide children to develop and employ their innate skills in a meaningful way, but we can be fairly skewed in assessing our children's strengths when blended with our own desires and fears.

One of my sons shows great artistic talent. Because my skills lie in the same arena, I jump at the chance to strengthen his artistic pursuits. It's a gift I understand and know how to cultivate. He also carries a strong sense of justice and can process concepts to the smallest of details. Because *these* particular traits ignite a fear of mine, I tend to ignore them. I worry that his passion for justice will manifest itself into his becoming the town crier, alarming authorities each and every time someone steps out of line. And one who verbally reasons through the minutiae of facts is not always welcome company. Therefore, I tend to discourage the latter traits and encourage the more acceptable ones in my eyes.

It's quite possible the days marked for his future will require he fight for justice or that his unquenchable thirst for reason will actually be used to clearly communicate truth. I may not fully comprehend the significance of my son's strengths, but I must learn to encourage him to develop those skills and trust time will reveal God's purposes. I need to faithfully bring him up in the way he should go.[1]

I consider this in the life of Joseph, one of Jacob's twelve sons. He is not one in the lineage of Christ (that falls to his brother Judah), but Joseph's role is so key to the preservation of Judah's family we cannot overlook him.

Jacob (whose name is changed by God to "Israel") deeply loved and favored Joseph. I'm sure Jacob and Rachel had dreams of what Joseph would become. To show his favor, Jacob blessed Joseph with a custom-made robe, separating him from his 11 brothers. As expected, this was not well received by his brothers, who already bore a grudge against their father's favorite son. In fact, it is written that his brothers *hated* him.[2]

Because Joseph was still a teenager, he was not involved in the demanding shepherding duties to the extent of his older brothers, but would report back to his father when they fell out of line. Then, to make matters more interesting, Joseph began having dreams where bundled wheat bowed down to him and celestial bodies gave him honor. The brothers were angered and even his father rebuked the "master of dreams" for his seeming lack of tact and relational sense. Dream interpretation was no gift to be developed in their eyes. Little did they know, it would play an integral part in their own survival.

Joseph's own flesh and blood plotted against him. In a moment of vengeful chaos, his brothers sold him into slavery. With a bloodstained robe as evidence, they lied to their father and reported Joseph killed. In

---

1 Prov. 22:6
2 Gen. 37:4

a single day's work, Joseph was now regarded *dead* to his own family.[3]

Joseph's circumstances seem out of control at this point. But God is ever present and continuously working, perfectly writing *His* story. As a slave, Joseph gained favor with his master, Potiphar, then was wrongly accused of taking advantage of his master's wife. Joseph became a prisoner under false charges, but then gained favor with the chief jailer. The king's cupbearer and baker soon joined Joseph in confinement.[4] Do we find it a coincidence then that both his cellmates had a dream on the same night and desired to know the meaning and that God moved Joseph to accurately interpret them? Are we astonished when, two years later, Pharaoh has two dreams troubling him to the point of searching his kingdom for an interpreter – a *master of dreams*?

> Pharaoh said to Joseph, "I have had a dream, but no one can interpret it; and I have heard it said about you, that when you hear a dream you can interpret it." Joseph then answered Pharaoh, saying, "It is not in me; *God* will give Pharaoh a favorable answer." (Gen. 41:15-16)

When Joseph interpreted the dreams, he foretold Egypt's immediate prosperity and imminent famine. By God's grace, Joseph offered sound advice for preparation and was placed in the highest position of power, just beneath the king himself. But it wasn't until desperation struck a *particular* family in the land in Canaan that we see this is more than a rags-to-riches story. God is preserving a branch, a Messianic one. Joseph's path of pain and grace delicately positioned him for when Jacob would send Joseph's brothers to Egypt to humbly ask for food. When the time came, Joseph couldn't deny God's intention.

> [Joseph] wept so loudly that the Egyptians heard it, and the household of Pharaoh heard of it. Then Joseph said to his brothers, "I am Joseph! Is my father still alive?" But his brothers could not answer him, for they were dismayed at his presence. Then Joseph said to his brothers, "Please come closer to me." And they

3 Gen. 37
4 Gen. 39, 40

> came closer. And he said, "I am your brother Joseph, whom you sold into Egypt. Now do not be grieved or angry with yourselves, because you sold me here... *God sent me* before you to preserve for you a remnant in the earth, and to keep you alive by a great deliverance. Now, therefore, it was not you who sent me here, but *God*." (Genesis 45:2-5,7-8)

And in one gracious rescue, God's covenant people were placed in a foreign land to live, away from Canaan – the promised land. Joseph had started out as a simple shepherd and was moved to a position of power under Pharaoh to deliver his family. In a grand reversal, God would now raise up another who would begin in a position of power and be moved to be a shepherd in Midian. This one would deliver God's family *from* Egypt *to* the Promised Land.

These are not circumstantial mishaps. God has called the shots from the beginning and the lines have fallen in precise and beautiful places for His redemption to be made perfect.

> The lot is cast into the lap, but its every decision is from the Lord. (Prov. 16:33)

> The Lord is the portion of my inheritance and my cup; You support my lot. The lines have fallen to me in pleasant places; indeed, my heritage is beautiful to me. (Ps. 16:5-6)

EXPERIENCE

Find blocks or items you can stack one on top of the other. Make predictions as to how many you can stack before the structure falls. Test to see if your predictions were true.

On what assumptions did you base your predictions? Were they accurate? What things were out of your direct control? Did something surprise you?

We can probably identify some points in our lives when our predictions took a turn. Sometimes we can hold so tightly to a self-written dream that we struggle to see God's perfect purpose for where we stand at the moment. We stack and stack and stack our lives to achieve a certain goal, but when someone pulls a block from down below, we fall in an undesirable place. Let's ask God for His perspective, that we would trust His providential hand.

Read Proverbs 16:3-4, Luke 16:10, and Romans 8:28.

DECEMBER 7

Judah

It happened at that time that Judah went down
from his brothers and turned aside.
Genesis 38:1 ESV

And now we actually have to take a step back and take a closer look at Judah. If you read Genesis 38 in context of the scriptures before and after, you may almost trip in your journey. As we observed Joseph's life, we practically sat on the sidelines cheering him along the way, giving "hurrahs" for the good guy and applauding God's blessing on our hero. But between Joseph being sold into slavery and the events that took place under Potiphar's roof, the narrative seems to come to a screeching halt, as if someone spliced in the wrong strip of film.

Under the sure inspiration of God, Moses intentionally wrote the account this way. He penned in a *silhouette* of sorts, taking something dark and pasting it directly on top of a white background. And like any contrast of that kind, you tend to ask why. The content of the chapter is terribly disturbing, but God has placed this here to stop us. It is not meant for us to awkwardly skip over. Remember that Christ's lineage is through Judah, not Joseph. This offshoot of the Christmas tree is bent and gnarly, but it is not a mistake.

We're given a little clue of the circumstances when we read the first verse of chapter 38: "Judah *went down*." Quite the understatement as we will soon discover. He left his family, and in the company of a friend who was not of his own way, headed to a foreign land. Then Judah married Shua, a woman from this distant land, and had three sons with her: Er, Onan, and Shelah. When the proper time came, Judah arranged for Er to marry Tamar. "But Er, Judah's firstborn, was evil in the sight of the Lord, so the Lord took His life" (Gen. 38:7).

Before we are tempted to feel as though God was overly harsh here, remember that sin has always resulted in death. We are not sure of the specifics of Er's sin, but God had a purpose for ending his life. According to custom, Judah commanded Onan, the son next in line, to take the firstborn's place and provide Tamar with children. This protected the widow and preserved the family's posterity. Later texts lay out the guidelines of this common Israelite practice:

> When brothers live together and one of them dies and has no son, the wife of the deceased shall not be married outside the family to a strange man. Her husband's brother shall... perform the duty of a husband's brother to her. It shall be that the firstborn whom she bears shall assume the name of his dead brother, so that his name will not be blotted out from Israel. (Deut. 25:5-6)

Onan, however, disobeyed this command and instead dishonored his deceased brother and Tamar. He abused the *privilege* and ignored the responsibility of taking Tamar to his bed as his wife. He acted with an abominable action, and the Lord took his life as well.[1]

The subject matter is troubling, but this is only the beginning. If God cannot be found *here*, then where is our hope? Perhaps that is why chapter 38 was placed in this particular spot, so that when we go

1 Gen. 38:8-10

through the valley of the shadow of death, we will see that He is with us.[2]

Tamar had mourned the death of two husbands, and Shelah (the youngest) who was next in line, was too young to take his brother's place. So Judah sent Tamar to live with her own father until Shelah was of age to marry her. Judah made Tamar a promise he intended to keep, but he worried that "[Shelah] *too* may die like his brothers" if he married Tamar (Gen. 38:11).

Can you imagine Tamar's broken heart? Her security lost. Her protection discarded. Her value abused. So much loss and waywardness. Where is God when the pieces shatter and fall and it hurts to even take a breath? Surely Tamar wondered when her promised time would come. Surely she grew suspicious. And sure enough, when Shelah came of age, what Tamar feared came to fruition. Tamar was abandoned by Judah's family.

Then Tamar did the unthinkable. She chose to secure her own justice and future through an act of deception. Aware of Judah's travels, she covered herself as a harlot and waited in his path. Vulnerable from mourning the death of his own wife, Judah made himself available to this "temple prostitute." Unknown to Judah, Tamar became pregnant from his seed and kept convicting evidence of the encounter in order to secure her revenge. Disgust cannot even begin to describe how we feel about what Tamar did in her deception.

So, what did Judah do? As the father to Tamar's baby, Judah was utterly broken. He couldn't just fix this. He would most certainly be a laughing stock. His leadership and honor would be compromised. But this time, instead of hiding or *going down* as Tamar had plotted for him, Judah declared his true state."[Tamar] is more righteous than I, inasmuch as I did not give her to my son Shelah" (Gen. 38:26).

Sin always leaves a mess in its wake. And the sinners drowning in its waters are left to discover the depth of their depravity. But for a second, let's fast forward to Jesus' earthly ministry. Remember how

2 Ps. 23:4

He touched the leper, and the dead girl, and the unclean? Remember how he feasted with the prostitutes, the tax collectors, and the sinners? Where there are ashes, He fashions a crown.[3] God boldly did the same with Judah and Tamar. For out of *this* relationship came a set of twins, one of whom was Perez, "a breach," from whom the line of the Messiah would break through. God chose Judah, from all the brothers.

We can now see that Chapter 38 is not out of place at all. This silhouette is perfectly placed for us to see a light shining in the darkness. We *need* to see that.

> For whatever was written in earlier times was written for our instruction, so that through perseverance and the encouragement of the Scriptures we might have hope. (Rom. 15:4)

EXPERIENCE

Cut out a large heart from a piece of paper. One by one, pass the heart around and have each person share one thing that has brought hurt, pain, or disappointment to their heart. As each person shares, tear a section off the heart and place it in a pile in front of everyone. Then read Isaiah 61:1-3 and 57:15. Tape the heart back together as you reiterate what God delights to do, the very thing Messiah is coming to do.

Once our hearts are broken, fear typically sets in and walls are built. But God is the mender of hearts. Will you take matters into your own hands or trust Him with the pieces?

---

3 Isa. 61:3

DECEMBER 8

Moses

Then Moses said to God, "Behold, I am going to the sons of Israel, and I will say to them, 'The God of your fathers has sent me to you.' Now they may say to me, 'What is His name?' What shall I say to them?" God said to Moses, "I AM WHO I AM ... Thus you shall say to the sons of Israel, The Lord, the God of your fathers, the God of Abraham, the God of Isaac, and the God of Jacob, has sent me to you.' This is My name forever, and this is My memorial name to all generations."
Exodus 3:13-15

Jacob's family thrived in Egypt under Joseph's provision. Although their covenant land was Canaan, they remained in this foreign land due to the famine and reunification of their family. Their blessing and numbers greatly increased, so much so that "the land was filled with them." As the years passed (centuries actually), we read that Pharaoh's throne was filled several times over.

> Now a new king arose over Egypt, who did not know Joseph. He said to his people, "Behold, the people of the sons of Israel are more and mightier than we. Come, let us deal wisely with them, or else they will multiply and in the event of war, they will also join themselves to those who hate us, and fight against us and depart from the land." (Exod. 1:8-10)

Context tells us that "deal wisely" meant *lord over*. This was Egypt's power play. Vanquish the Hebrews to slavery, and they would not realize their strength. However, when Pharaoh realized Plan A wasn't working as intended, he pursued Plan B: a genocidal mission. Pharaoh commanded "every [Hebrew] son who is born you are to cast into the Nile".[1] Decimate a gender, decimate a nation.

Let's pause here and consider the number of times to this point the mere existence of God's people has been threatened. Again and again God demonstrates that He is not terrorized by the schemes of man, nor of Satan. As Pharaoh signed the edict to bring death to the Hebrews, God brought onto the scene a little Hebrew boy to be His chosen vessel of deliverance.

Moses was hidden by his mother in the Nile, but was soon discovered by the Pharaoh's daughter. Enjoy the irony as this princess named him "Moses," which means *to draw out*. She saved his life by *drawing him out* of the Nile, just as God would call Moses to *draw His people out* of Egypt's bondage.[2]

As Moses grew up in the palace, he began to understand his roots and purpose were different from that of his royal family. One day, he acted in haste and killed an Egyptian to rescue another Hebrew. He fled to Midian, where he settled, married, and had a son.

God chose to introduce Himself anew to this long-forgotten *deliverer* one day while Moses was out shepherding. God began by referencing Himself as the Hebrews knew Him: "I am the God of your father, the God of Abraham, the God of Isaac, and the God of Jacob."

---

1 Exod. 1
2 Exod. 2

After initial introductions and describing the state of His people in bondage, God simply said, "I will send *you* to Pharaoh".[3]

Moses anticipated how the Hebrews would respond to God's impossible plan. He knew they would push against, even rebel at Moses as their leader. But God moved Moses out of the spotlight and gave him the name of the One leading this mission.

> God said to Moses, "I AM WHO I AM;" and He said, "Thus you shall say to the sons of Israel, "I AM has sent me to you."
> (Exod. 3:14)

The modern world is fogged with countless spiritual ideas. Many claim that "God" is an energy source or a general divine essence where all things receive their power. Others preach that "God" is some*thing* that can be channeled within through enlightenment or centeredness. Others conclude the idea of "God" as nothing more than humanity's way to comfort or anchor ourselves as we tackle the unknown. And still others characterize "God" a distant deity, unattached from the chaos on earth he created.

Moses identified with the same type of spiritual fog as it had settled on the Hebrews. For many years in bondage, God's voice seemed silent. "God" may have been more of an idea, a lost dream, a "God of their fathers," but no Father to them. Yet God makes a timely declaration to Moses. He names *Himself.* This is a significant revelation of His *personhood.* His name bears His character. He is active and present. This is the message God's people needed to hear.

I AM WHO I AM declares:

He exists. God is not dead. He is present and hears His people.

He has always existed, even before their fathers, meaning that He is greater than what they know. Jesus said, "Before Abraham was born, I am" (John 8:56-58).

He does not change. "Am" means He endures; He stays. *We* change because we lack information and understanding. But from the past, present, and future *He* lacks nothing; therefore, He need not

---

3 Exod. 3

change.

He is not bound by man. He is who He is. He exists and moves outside our control. Just as 1+1 will always equal 2 because it is a law outside our manufacturing – we cannot change it, only recognize it – so God *is.* He is the rule. Believing whatever we want about Him cannot change His essence.

He is all powerful. Not only does He declare the end, but He *sustains* the means by His might.

The revelation in His Name was something God's people were desperate to know when life appeared to hold no meaning other than suffering, when their cries seemed to fall on deaf ears. Might that be something *we* need to know as well?

> This is My name forever, and this is My memorial name to *all generations.* (Exod. 3:15)

By His mighty outstretched arm, God sent plagues on Egypt to denounce every false god and to deliver His people out from bondage. Through His servant Moses, God protected His people, preserved them with the Law, provided for their needs, and prepared them for the land that was promised.

From the beginning to the end, He continues to prove He is *exactly* what His name declares.

EXPERIENCE

Look up the meaning of your name. How significant is your name to you? Was it chosen to honor your family? Did the name embody a hope your parents had for you? Or was it simply popular at the time?

When God calls Himself *I AM*, He reveals what He has always been from which He does not waver.

> If we are faithless, He remains faithful, for He cannot deny Himself. (2 Tim. 2:13)

Take a look again at the meaning of His name I AM. What does this mean to you? Is this your perception of God or do you entertain a false assumption of who He is?

Read Psalm 9:10; 91:14 and Malachi 3:6 and thank the Lord for who He is.

DECEMBER 9

Rahab

For the Lord your God, He is God in heaven above and on earth beneath. Now therefore, please swear to me by the Lord, since I have dealt kindly with you, that you also will deal kindly with my father's household, and give me a pledge of truth, and spare my father and my mother and my brothers and my sisters, with all who belong to them, and deliver our lives from death.
Joshua 2:11-13

Moses took God's people to the boundaries of the promised land Canaan, which was occupied by foreign nations at the time. Moses sent in a dozen spies who returned to give a report of a bountiful land, yet it was populated with fearsome people and fortified cities. The Israelites were devastated. They had come all this way to view a place they couldn't possess. Joshua and Caleb, two of the spies, reminded the Hebrews of God's promise to give them the land, but to no avail.

The people chose to fear their enemies instead of trusting God. Devastatingly, their punishment for not trusting God was that their generation had to forfeit the privilege of occupying the promised land. Instead, they were forced to wander in the wilderness for 40 years until a new generation rose up.

Four decades later, the Israelites again found themselves at Canaan's border, just shy of the Jordan River. This new generation of Israelites was led by Joshua, Moses' servant and successor, and one of the original spies. Their first city to overtake was Jericho – strong and fortified. In preparation for attack, Joshua sent in two spies. To remain inconspicuous, they took refuge in the home of a harlot who lived within the city wall.

Consider the risk they took securing this hiding place among the enemy. But inasmuch as God had led these men to the right hiding place, He had also primed Rahab's heart. For after she redirected the king's men who were searching for the Israelite impostors, she rushed to address the spies she concealed among the flax on her roof.

> She came up to them on the roof, and said to the men, "I know that the Lord has given you the land, and that the terror of you has fallen on us, and that all the inhabitants of the land have melted away before you. For we have heard how the Lord dried up the water of the Red Sea before you when you came out of Egypt, and what you did to the two kings of the Amorites who were beyond the Jordan, to Sihon and Og, whom you utterly destroyed. When we heard it, our hearts melted and no courage remained in any man any longer because of you; for the Lord your God, He is God in heaven above and on earth beneath. Now, therefore, please swear to me by the Lord, since I have dealt kindly with you, that you also will...deliver our lives from death." (Josh. 2:8-13)

It's interesting that among the lists of honored men who are recorded during these crucial times – kings, spies, tribes, and leaders – we have such a detailed narrative of a non-Hebrew woman. And yet there is great significance as to why this conversation with the spies was included in the account. In the New Testament, both James and the Apostle Paul included Rahab in their *defense* of true faith. We must lean in and glean what she confessed when she spoke.

First, she knew she was on the enemy's side – a sure loss. She had resolved, like most in the city, that the Lord was on the side of the Hebrews. All of Jericho was aware of what God had done for His people. But one attribute set Rahab apart from her fellow citizens. Rahab *saw* the Truth. "The Lord your God, *He* is God in heaven above and on earth beneath" (Josh. 2:11b).

She declared what she knew, despite environmental factors, family influence, or rebellion all around. This is a miraculous, gracious work of God. She *recognized* He as *I AM.*

It brings to mind when in Matthew 16 Jesus asked His disciples in what ways the people identified Him. They responded "Elijah... Jeremiah... one of the prophets." He then asked, "Who do *you* say that I am?" to which Peter replied, "You are the Christ, the son of the Living God." Do you remember what Jesus said in response?

> And Jesus said to him, "Blessed are you, Simon Barjona, because flesh and blood did not reveal this to you, but My Father who is in heaven." (Matt. 16:17)

Like Peter, Rahab came to a *once-I-was-blind-but-now-I-see* place. Her eyes were opened to the truth of the One True God and her only hope for salvation. She was not just ascribing good luck to the Israelites who happened to have the stronger god on their side. Instead, she acknowledged that their God is *the* God who reigns supremely and sovereignly in the heavenly realm as on the earth.

Her actions at this point only confirm her faith. The spies agreed to spare her household, but she had to conceal the spies' whereabouts and tie a scarlet cord in the window. Thus her family would be saved during the siege. She obeyed because she believed her freedom rested in the hands of I AM. Rahab's faith was proven as she obeyed and acted accordingly.

> Was not Rahab the harlot also justified by works when she received

the messengers and sent them out by another way? (James 2:25)

And God was faithful. A scarlet thread waved a banner over her home on the day the Israelites took the city of Jericho. Rahab was spared and lived the rest of her days with God's people. How awesome is it to know that before the foundation of the world, God knew a Gentile prostitute who would one day *know Him*. Not only to be rescued, but as He intended, she would marry an Israelite and continue the Messianic line to the Savior Himself. A lovely, budding, foreign branch would be spliced in to this extraordinary Christmas tree, once again revealing His plan to save. Through God's scarlet line, One would come to take us out from within the walls of the Enemy and graft us in as His very own. What a marvelous heritage we have!

EXPERIENCE

Place a funnel on top of a clear glass. Gather a variety of objects (pencil, toy, wad of paper, coins, etc.). One by one drop each of these items into the funnel. Discuss why these objects will not fall through into the glass below. Now take sugar or salt and pour it in. Watch how the granules easily maneuver their way through the narrow path to the glass below. What makes it easy to pass through?

Rahab is the only household among an entire city who is saved. She and her family are the only ones who pass through and are preserved. Jesus Himself declares that the way is narrow for those who will find life.

> Enter through the narrow gate; for the gate is wide and the way is broad that leads to destruction, and there are many who enter through it. For the gate is small and the way is narrow that leads to life, and there are few who find it. (Matt. 7:13-14)

Though there is evidence to all,[1] it will only be the humble, the broken, who find the way of life, and that brokenness only comes from seeing the Truth. When we see God for who He truly is, then we see our condition accurately. And when we recognize our position, we are broken. He covers us by His great love and dies in our stead so that we are rescued from the wages we deserve.

Read John 3:36 and Colossians 1:13-14. Can you profess what you know to be true?

1 Rom. 2:20

DECEMBER 10

Boaz and Ruth

Then [Ruth] fell on her face, bowing to the ground and said to him, "Why have I found favor in your sight that you should take notice of me, since I am a foreigner?" Boaz replied to her, "All that you have done for your mother-in-law after the death of your husband has been fully reported to me, and how you left your father and your mother and the land of your birth, and came to a people that you did not previously know. May the Lord reward your work, and your wages be full from the Lord, the God of Israel, under whose wings you have come to seek refuge."
Ruth 2:10-12

The rescued Rahab joined God's covenant people and married Salmon, an Israelite. They had a son whom they named Boaz. Can you imagine him growing up listening to the stories of when his mother met the spies and tied the red thread on the window? Surely his father shared what it was like to see the walls of Jericho fall and how they were instructed to save Rahab when God gave them the city. I wonder what that family looked like, being different from other families, with a unique understanding of God's grace.

Boaz grew up to eventually settle in Bethlehem where he established great wealth and respect. He appreciated those serving under him and invested in the work that fell under his care. As Boaz was older in age and unmarried, we can assume his life was well into routine by this time. But one day as he came upon his field, he noticed a new face, an unexpected foreigner. He inquired about her.

> The servant in charge of the reapers replied, "She is the young Moabite woman who returned with Naomi from the land of Moab. And she said, 'Please let me glean and gather after the reapers among the sheaves.'" (Ruth 2:6-7)

Ruth was unknown to Boaz, but *Naomi*...now, this was a name he knew well for she was a close relative to him by way of her late husband, Elimelech. Perhaps out of a sense of responsibility, perhaps simply out of interest, Boaz responded to Ruth compassionately. He invited her to remain in his field, ensuring that she would find safety, favor, and plenty of grain to meet her and Noami's needs.

Ruth, this young foreigner, was overwhelmed. Only a short time ago, her husband had died in Moab, a nation known for its disdain for the Israelites and their God who had cursed the Moabites.[1] But when her beloved mother-in-law Naomi, an Israelite, decided to return back to Canaan after her husband and sons all died, Ruth committed to returning with her – to embrace Naomi's life, her home, her people, and most remarkably her God.[2] Ruth was aware that being a foreigner in this land, particularly a Moabite, would be a tremendous mark against her, but she was determined to honor her mother-in-law. The last thing she expected was to have kindness poured over her such as Boaz had in the field.

> Then she fell on her face, bowing to the ground and said to [Boaz], "Why have I found favor in your sight that you should take notice

1 Deut. 23:3-6
2 Ruth 1:16-18

of me, since I am a foreigner?" (Ruth 2:10)

Boaz relayed the report he had heard of her and then affirmed, "May the Lord reward your work, and your wages be full from the Lord, the God of Israel, under whose wings you have come to seek refuge" (Ruth 2:12). He knew she had placed herself under God's care. As a member of the Israelite family, one might come to *assume* God's favor. But as a foreigner, one would only come in humility to seek refuge under His wing. Boaz clearly saw Ruth's faith and took it upon himself to bless her.

It's important to study Naomi's intentions at this point. On returning to Bethlehem, she resolved herself as empty and afflicted. "Call me Mara," she demanded, viewing her life as *bitterness*.[3] She had left Canaan full and returned empty. No husband, no sons, no protection, no covering. But now an unforeseen course appeared in the night. Light broke into the darkness, for her widowed Moabite daughter-in-law had happened upon Boaz's field, and he took notice. Naomi prudently guided Ruth to humbly seek Boaz's favor. Though it all might seem just a shot in the dark, these are the places where God takes pleasure in shining.

How shocked Boaz must have been when one night sleeping on the threshing floor he awoke to find Ruth laying at his feet. As a *kinsman redeemer*, it was customary for the closest relative to buy or redeem a widowed relative so that she would not be left destitute. Boaz was quite aware of this custom, but he was also likely a generation older than Ruth and had honored Ruth by not assuming that position. Yet when Ruth positioned herself at his feet on this night and humbly requested to be taken under his wing, Boaz realized the hopeful prospect of a new role.

So here we behold three people. All of whom perceive they are past their time of blessing. All of whom are now experiencing a revelation of God's grace and character.

As a young adult, my view of salvation and God wavered and

3 Ruth 1:19-21

weakened. I believed, but I also felt He must be ashamed of me. As a Pharisee of sorts, I strove earnestly to win God's favor, working to obtain some sense of security. I taunted myself with my inability to do so and secretly lived under a blanket of condemnation.

I kept a list, tucked away during that time, of specific characteristics and virtues I desired in a future husband. I didn't know anyone who fit the bill because many of those statements were penned after some pain or heartache in a relationship with someone quite the opposite. The list wasn't long, but each attribute carried with it a personal reason. When I sat in the mire of my shame, I would look at the things on that list and feel so foolish. Embarrassed, I would read it then fold it back up. There was no possible way God would grant me any of it. Because of my sinfulness, I knew I had *passed* my time of blessing. Then Jeremy came.

Though I had seen him, I knew nothing of his character for several years until we wound up working together. I was quietly smitten with him, but knew I was only hoping for someone God wouldn't give *me*. As my friendship with Jeremy deepened, I grew afraid that he would be snatched away from me. I knew I did not deserve him. I waited apprehensively for something that would only confirm my reproof. However, one night on a walk we stopped to sit and look at the clear night sky. And it was in this moment God willfully opened that hidden list of mine. There, fixed within our conversation at the most unpredictable time, Jeremy spoke words straight off the page. Completely unaware, he shared the most precious of statements I had written that no one could know, except One.

I headed to my room that night wondering how that added up. This was not my idea of how God worked. Grace was being defined. I couldn't reason or take credit for it in any way; God had made it personal. He knew my heart and that I doubted He could or ever would bless me like this. And He lovingly unwrapped my list. He was giving this to me, not because I earned it, but because He loved me. My view of God and my salvation took a 180-degree turn that night.

For Boaz, Ruth, and Naomi, their meeting was almost too good to be true, too, but God's plan was in full motion. Boaz carried out the role of kinsman redeemer with integrity and married Ruth. Naomi eventually held her grandson in her lap, declaring that he was the restorer of her life and hope. This baby's name was Obed, who became the father of Jesse, who became the father of King David.[4]

Generation by generation, the Lord – the I AM – displays His redemption and creates such a hunger for salvation we can't help but wait to see how this will play out in this great story. We are not past the time of blessing, for "*when the fullness of the time came*, God sent forth His Son, born of a woman, born under the Law, so that He might *redeem* those who were under the Law, that we might receive the adoption as sons" (Gal. 4:4-5).

EXPERIENCE

Have everyone bring to the table one of their most prized possessions. Describe why this item has such great value. After each possession is described, give some time for others to make hypothetical offers on what it would cost to buy that particular item from that owner.

"Would you give that to me for ________ dollars?"

See if you could come to an agreeable amount or trade. It is quite possible that some things might be beyond a redeemable value, the owner unwilling to release the possession for anything in this life.

What value do *you* have in the eyes of God? Is there an acceptable price for your redemption? He does not redeem you by your works. That was unprofitable from the beginning. He does not redeem you by temporary means. Penance and devotion cannot cover us permanently. God redeems us by the sacrifice of His Son. And Hades itself cannot touch you for you are now under God's wing. God has provided for your redemption. He brought you out of the curse and made you His bride.

---

4 Ruth 4:13-17

> You were not redeemed with perishable things like silver or gold from your futile way of life inherited from your forefathers, but with precious blood, as of a lamb unblemished and spotless, the blood of Christ. (1 Pet. 1:18-19)

Read Psalm 40:1-5. Thank God for what He did for you because He loved you.

DECEMBER 11

Jesse

Thus Jesse made seven of his sons pass before Samuel. But Samuel said to Jesse, "The Lord has not chosen these." And Samuel said to Jesse, "Are these all the children?" And he said, "There remains yet the youngest, and behold, he is tending the sheep." Then Samuel said to Jesse, "Send and bring him; for we will not sit down until he comes here." So he sent and brought him in. Now he was ruddy, with beautiful eyes and a handsome appearance. And the Lord said, "Arise, anoint him; for this is he."
1 Samuel 16:10-12

As we follow the pattern of the Israelites, we can see that a change of circumstances does not change character. Since stepping foot out of Egypt, the Israelites continued to falter in faithfulness to their Deliverer. Forty years of wandering in the wilderness would seem sufficient to prune their wild ways, but when the bounty and victory of their new land was in their hands, they forgot who had provided it. Now once again a great nation in Canaan, their new *modus operandi* was to do what was right in their own eyes.[1] They arrogantly compromised with foreign nations and bartered their God for less demanding pagan options. At their request, God graciously established judges among the people, appointed leaders who kept order, enforced civility and adherence to the law, and worked to bring the focus back to Him. But God's people had blurred the lines that were meant to set them apart as a light to the nations. Now they sought to be *like the other nations.*[2]

At the right time, God appointed Samuel to be a prophet to His people in order to clearly and consistently broadcast messages of repentance and promise. When the Philistines took the ark of the covenant and sought to defeat the Israelites, it was the prophet Samuel who proclaimed that if the people would rid themselves of idolatry, God's protection would be sure when they faced their great enemy. And as promised, God's mighty hand was no match for the Philistines. After their great victory, Samuel immediately took a stone and named it *Ebenezer* declaring, "Thus far the Lord has helped us." The Lord stayed the fury of the Philistines all the days of Samuel.[3]

Isn't it fascinating how even when we live in triumphant stability, we will still convince ourselves we can find rest elsewhere?[4]

> Then all the elders of Israel gathered together and came to Samuel… "Now appoint a king for us to judge us *like all the nations.*" But the thing was displeasing in the sight of Samuel when they said, "Give us a king to judge us." And Samuel prayed to the Lord. The Lord said to Samuel, "Listen to the voice of the people in regard to all that they say to you, for they have not rejected you, but *they have rejected Me* from being king over them. Like all the deeds which they have done since the day that I brought them up from Egypt even to this day – in that they have forsaken Me and served other gods – so they are doing to you also." (1 Sam. 8:4-8)

So at the request of the people and the Lord's cautionary consent,

1 Judg. 21:25
2 Deut. 17:14
3 1 Sam. 7:11-14
4 Prov. 14:12

Samuel anointed Israel's first king – S*aul.* Tall and handsome, this leader was outwardly pleasing and appealing to the nation of Israel. But as they continued to face their enemies, Saul repeatedly wrestled with God's will versus the requests of the people. Eventually, Saul chose to follow the will of the people.

> Then Saul said to Samuel, "I have sinned; I have indeed transgressed the command of the Lord and your words, because I *feared the people* and listened to *their* voice." (1 Sam. 15:24)

The consequences were dire. Because Saul had disregarded the Lord's instruction, the Lord rejected Saul as king over Israel. Samuel grieved over the failure of this leader, but God was still at work. He revealed to Samuel, "I will send you to Jesse the Bethlehemite, for I have selected a king for *Myself* among his sons" (1 Sam. 16:1). And so let's step back and find this line in the family tree. *Jesse* is the grandson of Ruth and Boaz in Bethlehem.

When Samuel arrived in Bethlehem to identify God's chosen one, he simply stated his purpose was to make a sacrifice to the Lord. He invited the elders of the city, along with Jesse and his sons, to join him. One by one the proud father introduced his sons before Samuel. Seven sons were presented, and God said "no" to each. Surely confused, Samuel asked if Jesse had any other children, to which Jesse indifferently responded that his youngest was currently out in the fields watching the flocks. Samuel insisted that *this* son be presented. You can imagine everyone's surprise when God pulled Samuel to his feet and said, "Anoint him; for this is he" to the ruddy-faced juvenile, David.[5]

God's people, His anointed people, rejected their name and desired to mimic the very nations from which God had set them apart. The Philistines and other enemies were breathing down their necks. What they *wanted* was a hero. What they *needed* was to return to the Lord. And God could have chosen a military genius or a priest-like figure to reform the nation, but His way was not the people's way. No one would have chosen the shepherd David, not even his father Jesse. But from

5 1 Sam. 16:4-12

this overlooked shoot on this particular family tree, God planned to bring about a Savior.[6]

> "God sees not as man sees, for man looks at the outward appearance, but the Lord looks at the heart." (1 Sam. 16:7)

EXPERIENCE

Take three bowls and one small item. Place the bowls upside down and have everyone look away while you place the item underneath one of the bowls. Let each person take a turn guessing which bowl is hiding the object. Have them explain why they made their particular choice. Ask how they could make a *sure* choice. Since they did not *see* you place the object underneath, perhaps they could ask the person who *did see*.

Consider the decisions before you or ones you've made in the recent past. Choosing the right way, even when we want what is best, can be difficult to discern. We make pro and con lists. We ask our family and friends. We watch to see what others have done. Or we may just take a shot in the dark. The truth is we cannot see the greater picture, but there is One who does. He is the one we must ask. He is the One Who Sees.[7]

We look so much to the outward appearance of people and circumstances, but God looks at the heart. His way is not always the choice of the people. But when He directs in one way, we can be sure He will equip and provide.

Read Psalm 106 for a record of Israel's repetitive sin and God's continuous mercy.

---

6 Isa. 11:1
7 Gen. 16:13

DECEMBER 12

David, the Musician

Behold, I have seen a son of Jesse the Bethlehemite who is a skillful musician, a mighty man of valor, a warrior, one prudent in speech, and a handsome man; and the Lord is with him.
1 Samuel 16:18

There are numerous facets of David described in scripture. Not only is he a key figure in the line of Christ, but his blend of gifts is fascinating. David doesn't match the stereotypes of a warrior and leader. As a youth, he used his hands to kill a bear, a lion, and even a giant Philistine. But he also applied those gifted hands to create music on the harp. And though this "son of Jesse" was bold and strong in speech, he was also known to retreat to write poetic words of praise, vulnerability, and lament.

Half of the songs in the book of Psalms are written by David. Imagine hearing him play and sing them! Many of his refrains resounded with shouts of joy, declaration, and thanksgiving. And other songs exposed a heart wrestling with fear, confession, and desperation. His hymns laid the full breadth of him bare. From the days of his youth to his deathbed, this "skilled musician" shared a transparency with the Lord where every door of his heart was wedged ajar for God's invited inspection.

King Saul first commissioned "the sweet psalmist of Israel" to use his prolific musical ability to calm Saul in his distress.[1] Accompanied by his harp, David was invited onto the royal stage. Much would take place however before David actually wore the crown that Samuel had anointed to him.

David's song-writing career begins to bud under these unique circumstances. His popularity grew among the people for he was more skilled, brave, and wise than any of the king's men. Saul's jealousy escalated until anger eventually took root and betrayal ensued. Fleeing a spear in the midst of a performance, David's comfortable circumstances transitioned to fleeing for his life. Leaving his "brother" and wife, both children of King Saul, he succumbs to hiding and waiting on God's anointing.[2] So in the midst of this unstable tangle of circumstances he penned this song:

> Deliver me from my enemies, O my God; set me securely on high away from those who rise up against me. Deliver me from those who do iniquity and save me from men of bloodshed. For behold, they have set an ambush for my life; fierce men launch an attack against me, not for my transgression nor for my sin, O Lord, for no guilt of mine, they run and set themselves against me. Arouse Yourself to help me, and see!... But as for me, I shall sing of Your strength; yes, I shall joyfully sing of Your lovingkindness in the morning, for You have been my stronghold and a refuge in the day of my distress. (Ps. 59:1-4, 16)

Through an incredible series of events, David eventually became

1 1 Sam. 16:14-23
2 1 Sam. 18, 19

the king of Israel, but only at God's appointed time 15 years later.[3] "He gives great deliverance to His king, and shows lovingkindness to His anointed, to David and his descendants forever," he sang in prayer.[4] This young king went to war with the Philistines and many of their neighboring nations, defeated Israel's enemies, and regained Israel's rightful inheritance.

Not all his songs were choruses of praise. Many were strung in minor chords of devastation and failure. Though David's leadership proved impeccable, he was not a symbol of perfection. Many years after taking the throne at a time when his men were in battle, David remained home and took another man's wife. She became pregnant. To cover his sin, David manipulated her husband's marching orders and placed him in harm's way to have him killed. David then took Bathsheba as his wife – an attempt to remove the implicating guilt. David thought he was free and clear – the truth of his transgression remained unknown to Israel, but Nathan the prophet confronted David's sin.[5] In confession, David sang out to God:

> Behold, You desire truth in the innermost being, and in the hidden part You will make me know wisdom. Purify me with hyssop, and I shall be clean; wash me, and I shall be whiter than snow. Make me to hear joy and gladness, let the bones which You have broken rejoice. Hide Your face from my sins and blot out all my iniquities. Create in me a clean heart, O God, and renew a steadfast spirit within me. Do not cast me away from Your presence and do not take Your Holy Spirit from me. Restore to me the joy of Your salvation and sustain me with a willing spirit. (Ps. 51:6-12)

No matter the failure or discipline, faith or victory, David turned to his King and pursued God passionately. Then by the work of the Spirit, he would instruct his heart. "Bless the Lord, O my soul, and all that is within me, bless His holy name. Bless the Lord, O my soul, and

---

3 2 Sam. 5:1-5
4 Ps. 18:50
5 2 Sam. 11:1-12:14

forget none of His benefits," he commanded himself in song.[6] He did not merely lead the people by his scepter, but compelled them also in metered verse.

> I will bless the Lord at all times; His praise shall continually be in my mouth. My soul will make its boast in the Lord; the humble will hear it and rejoice. O magnify the Lord with me, and let us exalt His name together... Come, you children, listen to me; I will teach you the fear of the Lord. (Ps. 34:1-3, 11)

The Psalms hold David's portfolio of music written in response to the One he loved more than anyone or anything else. "You are my hiding place; You preserve me from trouble; You surround me with songs of deliverance" (Ps. 32:7). Those songs continued to be sung by God's people, looking forward to a day when they would sing them in presence of the King of Kings. But would they be willing to sing them to another Shepherd?

EXPERIENCE

Have you ever listened to a song and felt as though that songwriter perfectly interpreted your deepest thoughts? Sing or share the words to a song that is personal to you. Why is this song so significant?

What might be the first lines of a song you would write describing your perspective right now? Would it be written to God or to others? How difficult would it be for you to share your words publicly?

Read 2 Samuel 22:1 and 23:1. Isn't it incredible that we've received more revelation of God Himself through a hymnbook written by an Israelite king?

---

6 Ps. 103:1-2

DECEMBER 13

David, the King

They asked for a king, and God gave them Saul the son of Kish, a man of the tribe of Benjamin, for forty years. After He had removed him, He raised up David to be their king, concerning whom He also testified and said, "I have found David the son of Jesse, a man after My heart, who will do all my will."
Acts 13:17-22

Hidden behind flourishing branches, a ruddy growth became the focal point. God was not looking on the outward appearance when He chose David. This branch, though just a shoot, would be developed into a foundational bough giving strength and direction to our persevering Christmas tree. Though his brothers may have burned with envy over their youngest brother being divinely chosen, they would have had second thoughts if they had to walk the *life* also chosen for him. This royal branch grew unseemly knots amid the green and bore threatening scars through his years. But David grew confident of God's choice and

His pruning:

> You know when I sit down and when I rise up... Even before there is a word on my tongue, behold, O Lord, You know it all. You have enclosed me behind and before, and laid Your hand upon me... in Your book were all written the days that were ordained for me, when as yet there was not one of them. (Ps. 139)

The days penned for David included leaving his father Jesse to serve King Saul, defeating the feared Goliath, befriending the king's son, and fleeing for his life. It was written that he would fight the Philistines repeatedly in victory, command the nation's army, and become the most revered reigning king of God's chosen people. During his reign the ark of the covenant was brought to Jerusalem and plans were made for building a temple for God. But those ordained days also encompassed losing confidants, wives, and children, and being betrayed by those closest to him. David committed adultery and murder, then suffered corruption and immoral acts within his own family. Through it all, he knew God's hand was on him, enclosing him before and behind.

When Saul deviated from obeying God's command, Samuel sadly informed the king that God would not allow his reign to endure. Instead, "the Lord has sought out for Himself a man after His own heart" to rule the people.[1] King David would do "all His will."[2] When we hear this we might be tempted to elevate David to some form of superior righteousness or perfection that *deserved* such a high regard from the Lord. But King David's last words would beg you to consider otherwise.

> Now these are the last words of David. David the son of Jesse declares, the man who was raised on high declares, the anointed of the God of Jacob, and the sweet psalmist of Israel, "The Spirit of the Lord spoke by me, and His word was on my tongue. The God of Israel said, the Rock of Israel spoke to me, 'he who rules over

1 1 Sam. 13:13-14
2 Acts 13:22

> men righteously, who rules in the fear of God, is as the light of the morning when the sun rises, a morning without clouds, when the tender grass springs out of the earth, through sunshine after rain.' Truly is not my house so with God? For He has made an everlasting covenant with me, ordered in all things, and secured; for all my salvation and all my desire, will He not indeed make it grow?" (2 Sam. 23:1-5)

David was introduced not as king, but as a *son of Jesse.* The final credits of the sweet psalmist's life did not puff the crown, but pointed to the One who anointed him. God had given David every word he wrote or spoke. His successful reign hinged solely on his fear of God. That was where Israel's hope would be found. Not in David's reputation, wisdom, bravery, talent, or favor, but on nothing less than the Lord Himself. To be *a man after God's own heart* was to entrust everything, including his own life, to the Sovereign King.

David was not perfect, but he knew God was. David could not battle the Philistine alone, but he knew God could. David could not preserve his own life, but he trusted God would. David could not secure the crown for he was not Saul's son, but by divine authority God would. David could not remove the stain of his sin, but he sought the One who could restore. David could not create gladness from mourning, but he knew the One who could breathe life from dust. He saw the Lord as the *only* One who had the right to anything under his care. "You are my Lord; I have no good besides You" (Ps. 16:2).

Centuries after David's time, Paul presented to the Jews in Pisidian Antioch an incredible synopsis of history to explain where their hope was found. Paul began with the Israelites' captivity in Egypt and moved right up to David's reign. It was *this* king's rule they longed for again. But Paul succinctly passed through history right over David to the main point of his confession:

> [God] also testified and said, "I have found David the son of Jesse, a man after My heart, who will do all My will." From the descendants of this man, according to promise, *God has brought to*

Israel a Savior, Jesus." (Acts 13:22-23)

This kingly branch, though beautiful in form and strength, would not rest on David but would extend through seasons of darkness, destruction, and restoration to bear a Righteous Branch who would rule all the nations.[3] It was for *this* Sovereign that David lived his life.

EXPERIENCE

Make a list of significant occurrences that have taken place this year. Include internal and external transitions, victories and defeats, and times of rest or struggle. Read each point on the timeline, but following each event repeat the words: "His lovingkindness endures forever!"

Sometimes called "The Great Hallel," Psalm 136 is read together at the yearly Passover meal to remind each other of God's goodness, faithfulness, and love for His people, even through their history which bears both well-being and calamity. After every line in the Psalm, in unison we proclaim "For His lovingkindness endures forever!"

Read Psalm 136. May we trust our story is all about Him, the author and perfecter of our faith.

---

3 Ps. 2:6-8

DECEMBER 14

Solomon

Now, O Lord my God, You have made Your servant king in place of my father David, yet I am but a little child; I do not know how to go out or come in. Your servant is in the midst of Your people which You have chosen, a great people who are too many to be numbered or counted. So give Your servant an understanding heart to judge Your people to discern between good and evil. For who is able to judge this great people of Yours?
1 Kings 3:7-9

I have just finished reading two books back-to-back. Though different in genre, they are similar in character. Both authors invest chapter upon chapter to skillfully evolve significant struggle and mystery among the characters. Both stories develop to give glimpses of hope, but tragically both end without redemption of any kind. On the last few pages, the reader is urged to accept that life merely exists and hope is simply a facade. The content prompted me to research the authors, who both were praised for their *insightful* grasp of life's reality. But, is this reality?

Does life honestly amount to pointlessly making the most of the mess?

As you study King Solomon's life, you may start to feel as though you are reading one of those despairing stories. Just as the candle's light grows from a flicker to a flame, it seems to get blown out. The master plan appears to be unraveling. Do not despair, fellow reader, because God will have the last word. He is the writer. *He* is brilliant. Just when we determine that the only heroic act has irreversibly been foiled, the preeminent Hero steps in.

Not long after Solomon began his reign, he had a dream. The Lord promised to give Solomon something of his own desire, and Solomon requested one thing: wisdom. More precisely, he asked for a "hearing heart,"[1] one capable of listening to the Source of all wisdom and then judging correctly what is good and what is evil. This pleased the Lord that Solomon would yearn for applied knowledge above all other things, and He blessed Solomon well above his petition.[2] Solomon became a great and wise judge both of the people under his authority and in foreign relations.

Like his father, Solomon was also a talented writer, composing 3000 proverbs and 1005 songs. His writings were filled with principles, insight, wisdom, and perspective paralleled by no other. Song of Solomon, Proverbs, and Ecclesiastes were all written by Solomon.

David desired to build a temple, but the Lord determined this worthy task would be reserved for Solomon's reign. The temple, which took seven years for Solomon to build, was an amazing structure built of stone and cedar, completely overlaid with gold from top to bottom. It was to be a place of communion between God and His people. The temple, with its layout, instruments, restrictions, and dimensions, symbolically pointed to what God would eventually accomplish by His Son's sacrifice for those who would believe. God chose Solomon to take on this great task and equipped him to do so.[3]

Solomon's reign extended 40 years and is known as the "golden

---

1 1 Kings 3:9
2 1 Kings 3:7-13
3 1 Chron. 28:2-11

age of Israel," the nation's highest regard. Under Solomon's rule, Israel enjoyed the greatest peace and prosperity in all its history, even to present-day. Solomon and the nation grew exponentially in wealth and territory. David had spent most of his 40-year reign battling to defeat the neighboring enemy nations. By contrast, Solomon spent most of his 40-year reign living from the harvest of those efforts. "But now the Lord my God has given me rest on every side; there is neither adversary nor misfortune" (1 Kings 5:4).

Make no mistake though, when there is an absence of battle and struggle, the awareness of the cost of peace and prosperity tends to fade from memory. And when we forget the cost, our guard is laid low. An opportunistic enemy will not miss this turn. Though it seems unbalanced, God had a purpose for this generational switch of circumstances.

God had declared that the nation of Israel was to serve Him alone and set themselves apart from the surrounding pagan nations. In addition, they were called to be a light to those nations, directing them toward God. However, over 400 years earlier as His people were about to enter the Promised Land, the Lord revealed that one day they would ask for a king like the other nations, and He pronounced a warning to that future king.

> When you enter the land which the Lord your God gives you, and you possess it and live in it, and you say, "I will set a king over me like all the nations who are around me," you shall surely set a king over you whom the Lord your God chooses, one from among your countrymen you shall set as king over yourselves; you may not put a foreigner over yourselves who is not your countryman. Moreover, he shall not multiply horses for himself... He shall not multiply wives for himself, or else his heart will turn away; nor shall he greatly increase silver and gold for himself." (Deut. 17:14-17)

Before his death, David instructed Solomon, "Keep the charge of the Lord your God, to walk in His ways, to keep His statutes, His commandments, His ordinances, and His testimonies" (1 Kings 2:3).

Unfortunately, Solomon sowed seeds in wayward efforts to create political alliances, keep the peace, and secure the nation's stability. Those seeds took root and gradually led to the nation crumbling at the end of his years.

> Now King Solomon loved many foreign women... from the nations concerning which the Lord had said to the sons of Israel, "You shall not associate with them, nor shall they associate with you, for they will surely turn your heart away after their gods." Solomon held fast to these in love. He had seven hundred wives, princesses, and three hundred concubines, and his wives turned his heart away. For when Solomon was old, his wives turned his heart away after other gods; and his heart was not wholly devoted to the Lord his God, as the heart of David his father had been. (1 Kings 11:1-4)

The number of foreign wives Solomon had is dumbfounding. What he probably saw as a strong move to seal the deal in foreign relations between Israel and other nations actually became the pulled thread that unraveled him. Just as God warned, to covenant oneself with those who have no allegiance to the One True God will cause sure unfaithfulness to your First Love. Solomon conceded to his wives' demands to build shrines and high places to the pagan gods they worshipped. He became wise in his own eyes and did not keep God's statutes as God commanded. In the end, the wise man acted quite foolishly.

It is Solomon who wrote, "The fear of the Lord is the beginning of knowledge; fools despise wisdom and instruction."[4] Solomon began his years with his heart hungry to hear God's way, but concluded his days with a divided heart.

> So the Lord said to Solomon, "Because you have done this, and you have not kept My covenant and My statutes, which I have commanded you, I will surely tear the kingdom from you, and will give it to your servant. Nevertheless I will not do it in your days for

4 Prov. 1:7

> the sake of your father David, but I will tear it out of the hand of your son." (1 Kings 11:11-12)

You may feel like slamming the book shut. How could it end this way? For all that was built from David's kingdom, we find it crumbling under his son's leadership. "Vanity of vanities! All is vanity." The wise king over Israel had set his mind to explore knowledge, test pleasure, accumulate wealth, and feed his ambition, but he was left wanting. Another story with lingering despair. All is vanity. But when the son of David grew weary of his fruitless pursuit, he preached a final proverb.

> The conclusion, when all has been heard, is: fear God and keep His commandments, because this applies to every person. For God will bring every act to judgment, everything which is hidden, whether it is good or evil. (Eccles. 12:13)

Do not close the book on this story. Remember who calls light out of darkness, who has declared the end from the beginning. One day a wonderful Counselor from the line of David would establish His kingdom. This Prince of Peace would come having nothing, even borrowing a donkey for his triumphal entry, in order to redeem His bride to whom He would be faithful forever.[5]

A King is coming, and His kingdom will stand forever!

EXPERIENCE

Complete the sentence: *If I only had* ________________, *then I could* ________________________.

I'm sure we could come up with a long list of situations and outcomes that would suit us well. And though there may be some ideas we would confess as selfish, it is quite possible that most of what we considered has good purpose intended.

5 2 Cor. 8:9, John 12:14, Eph. 5:25-27

Many times our aspirations spring from our desire to make something right or to fix what seems wrong now. *If I had more money, then I could get out of debt. If I had a bigger home, then I could open my home more or have more children.* Those resolutions and outcomes can be very pure, but our "if onlys" can be very one-dimensional. We don't see the workings of each aspect of our lives and the cause and effect of those details. We also don't soberly assess our lives to see that having what we think would be good could actually be our greatest temptation – a devastating tool for the enemy's use.

The Lord has a very poignant if/then statement for Solomon:

> "*If* you walk in My ways, keeping My statutes and commandments, as your father David walked, *then* I will prolong your days."
> (1 Kings 3:14)

May our hopes rest on the Lord enriching our days. Whether the Lord gives us the means we think would be best or takes us on a completely different path, will we be content to trust He is good and He is *for* our good? Read Solomon's words in Proverbs 3:1-12.

DECEMBER 15

Evil Kings

He walked in all the sins of his father which he had committed before him;
and his heart was not wholly devoted to the Lord his God,
like the heart of his father David.
1 Kings 15:3

The son of Solomon, Rehoboam, assumed the crown after his father's death. As one would expect, the people approached him immediately with their concerns and desires, hoping for change. They requested he lessen the burdens they had long endured under Solomon's reign. All the growth and building that had taken place under his rule had been supported largely by heavy taxing and forced labor. The people needed a break. Rehoboam, newly installed as king, faced his first major policy decision: *To unburden or not to unburden*, that is the question.

We do the same with our leaders. We approach our newly elected leaders with a laundry list of changes we hope they'll implement immediately to make our lives better. Politics are tricky. Decisions must be made on more than current social pressures; the political agencies must consider forthcoming threats, political gain, and national stability. Concessions or rulings are at times made for the purpose of paving a way for prospective movements, which might remain unseen. So we can approach this impasse by either seeking the One who knows the future or pursuing man's idea of what *seems* right. And when our governing authorities work to *please* man, we will surely find our snare.[1]

Rehoboam consulted two sets of advisers. One group had served his father, and the other group was composed of younger men who had served Rehoboam in his youth. Solomon's advisers requested he speak and act kindly toward the people, listen to them, and secure their faithfulness. His personal advisors, however, urged him to increase the demands on the people to secure his own authority and power. Rehoboam chose the latter. You can almost guess what happened.[2]

A significant split occurred during Rehoboam's reign. Half of his kingdom, 10 tribes, left under the leadership of Jeroboam (retaining the name *Israel*), and two tribes remained (assuming the name *Judah*). Jerusalem, the central capital and location of the temple, was in Judah. Israel created its own places of worship. A feud arose between the divided tribes, and the great nation continued its downfall. One could blame Rehoboam for the eventual destruction of the great nation, but there is a long line of kings that are to blame for the people turning away from God. Before the people even entered the Promised Land, God reiterated His promise to them through Moses:

> I have set before you today life and prosperity, and death and adversity; in that I command you today to love the Lord your God, to walk in His ways and to keep His commandments and His statutes and His judgments, that you may live and multiply, and that the Lord your God may bless you in the land where you are entering to possess it. But if your heart turns away and you will not obey, but are drawn away and worship other gods and serve them,

---

1 Prov. 29:25
2 1 Kings 12:1-15

> I declare to you today that you shall surely perish... I call heaven and earth to witness against you today, that I have set before you life and death, the blessing and the curse. So choose life in order that you may live, you and your descendants. (Deut. 30:15-19)

Unfortunately, man's heart is drawn to seek its own way. Our default is to take the path with the least conflict and struggle. We plant little seeds of disobedience that will most assuredly grow unless they are pulled out at the roots. Herein lies the problem with the diseased branch of kings growing from both Judah's and Israel's royal line.

As goes the leader, so goes the nation. Solomon permitted the idols and shrines of his wives' pagan cultures. His son Rehoboam "did evil for he did not set his heart to seek the Lord." His son Abijah "walked in all the sins of his father."[3] While there were a handful of Judah's kings who turned their hearts to the Lord and worked diligently to restore a right focus among God's people, the majority of kings did what was evil, each growing in intensity from the one who came before. It is a sad decline.

Jehoram, the fifth king of Judah, was driven by fear and power. He killed his six brothers to secure the throne and even married the daughter of King Ahab (an evil king of Israel).[4] When Ahaziah, his son, took the crown "he walked in the ways of the house of Ahab, for his mother was his counselor to do wickedly."[5] Paganism increased and pursuing a true God seemed archaic. By the time Ahaz took the throne (11th king of Judah), we are appalled by the depth to which the nation has fallen. Ahaz *himself* built pagan shrines, sought pagan aid, sacrificed his sons alive to pagan gods, imported idols from neighboring lands, erected a pagan altar near the temple, and closed the sacred temple for worship.[6] His descendants, Manasseh and Amon, followed suit. They were quite the contrast from the beloved David. The kings walked in their malicious ways and led the nation to play the harlot to their God.

---

3 2 Chron. 12:14, 1 Kings 15:3
4 2 Chron. 21:12-15
5 2 Chron. 22:3
6 2 Kings 16

In doing so, the people refused the blessing and became recipients of God's anger that ultimately led to their demise.

Where was the light of Judah and Israel? Whose god did they serve? It had become a dark place. Like in the days of Noah, shouldn't the Lord wipe them from the face of the earth? They mocked the Lord in their pride and the people did not deserve His deliverance. Certainly they did not deserve His grace. They did not deserve... *they* did not deserve... *we* do not deserve... *I* do not deserve.

In the midst of this story, can we see the depravity of our own souls? The "mind set on the flesh is hostile toward God" and we cannot please Him in this way. Just as Moses delivered God's message of blessing and curse, we have gone the way of the curse. "Cursed is everyone who does not abide by all things written in the book of the Law, to perform them" (Gal. 3:10). So, what are we to do? Where is our hope? How can we be saved from this darkness, from this curse?

> Christ *redeemed us from the curse* of the Law, having *become a curse for us* – for it is written, "Cursed is everyone who hangs on a tree" – in order that in Christ Jesus *the blessing of Abraham might come* to the Gentiles, so that we would receive the promise of the Spirit through faith." (Gal. 3:13-14)

EXPERIENCE

Plan to get up early and observe the sunrise. Have you ever considered why we dote over the sunrise with *ooohs* and *ahhhs* and not carry on so during the rest of the sunny hours of the day?

Consider the contrast of the morning sun to the darkness just moments before. Give attention to the colors – pinks, purples, blues, and golds. God beckons us to take notice of its arrival, doesn't He?

God even handles the darkness for His glory. His coming is as sure as the dawn. After the night, we see His brilliance, His depth, His color and we praise Him for coming! He has never changed; it's just that a timely contrast made us see Him, didn't it?

Sing "I Heard the Bells on Christmas Day." The song shares this same observation of God's brilliance in contrast to the dark.

And in despair I bowed my head
"There is no peace on earth," I said,
"For hate is strong and mocks the song
of peace on earth, good will to men."

Then pealed the bells more loud and deep:
"God is not dead, nor doth He sleep;
The wrong shall fail, the right prevail
With peace on earth, good will to men." [7]

Read the reality of this contrast in John 3:19-21.

---

7 (Words: Longfellow, Henry Wadsworth. *Christmas Bells*. 1864. Music: Calkin, John Baptiste. *I Heard the Bells on Christmas Day*. 1872.)

DECEMBER 16

Isaiah

Then I said, "Woe is me, for I am ruined! Because I am a man of unclean lips, and I live among a people of unclean lips; for my eyes have seen the King, the Lord of hosts." Then one of the seraphim flew to me with a burning coal in his hand, which he had taken from the altar with tongs. He touched my mouth with it and said, "Behold, this has touched your lips; and your iniquity is taken away and your sin is forgiven." Then I heard the voice of the Lord, saying, "Whom shall I send, and who will go for Us?" Then I said, "Here am I. Send me!"

Isaiah 6:5-8

As a mother, I know the differences between my kids and how that dictates the manner in which I address their rebellious self-will. With my oldest, he is a terrific actor. He knows what we expect and can perform brilliantly. I have to uncover the hidden motive in logical ways. My daughter will not budge when confronted about disobedience, but must be given the facts and then left alone. After battling with it for some time, she will typically step out and voluntarily confess her wrong. My youngest however has to experience some type of loss before he sees the source of downfall. Counting the cost brings him to his senses. Discipline methods are unpleasant to administer at the time, but I'm willing for the sake of their maturity. My intent is to first help my children understand their folly, bring about a proper humilty, and guide them in a change of heart and behavior. As God's children rebel, I notice Him uniquely loving and correcting them in similar fashion.

Right in the middle of Judah's line of kings, Uzziah assumed the throne. Following two kings whose fickle ways turned to evil at the end of their reigns, Uzziah's lengthy rule was a refreshing era. As long as he remained faithful to the Lord, the nation experienced great prosperity both on the battlefront and in expansion efforts. Uzziah's fame grew among the nations and his hopeful people. But this symbol of hope fell from the throne as Uzziah was plagued with leprosy to the day he died.

In the same year as Uzziah's death, a messianic prophet found himself in a throne room, but not of an earthly king. Isaiah had a vision of the Lord seated on a high throne in the temple as angels reverberated "Holy, Holy, Holy!" over the Sovereign's head. Isaiah trembled at the realization that he was face-to-face with a holy God whose judgments are both severe and right. The prophet was profoundly made aware of the chasm between himself and this Righteous King, sin barring any favor.

The only avenue that allowed communion between the trembling Isaiah and the lofty One was a cleansing work performed by God's hand.[1] *Man* must be changed in order to have access to this King. And the words of God set Isaiah aflame to deliver over and over the prophecy of a felled Christmas tree and its holy stump. He decreed the Mighty One would "lob off the boughs with a terrible crash" but redemption would arise. A branch would shoot from its roots: "the stem of Jesse."[2]

---

1 Isa. 6
2 Isa. 10:33-11:1

Isaiah prophesied during the reigns of Uzziah, Jotham, Ahaz, and Hezekiah. The message of judgment he shared was directed to both the people and the kings. Isaiah addressed sin, idolatry, and their reliance on other nations instead of on God Himself.

> "Woe to the rebellious children," declares the Lord, "who execute a plan, but not Mine, and make an alliance, but not of My Spirit, in order to add sin to sin; who proceed down to Egypt without consulting Me, to take refuge in the safety of Pharaoh and to seek shelter in the shadow of Egypt! Therefore the safety of Pharaoh will be your shame." (Isa. 30:1-3)

> Then the Lord said, "Because this people draw near with their words and honor Me with their lip service, but they remove their hearts far from Me, and their reverence for Me consists of tradition learned by rote... Woe to those who deeply hide their plans from the Lord, and whose deeds are done in a dark place, and they say, 'Who sees us?' or 'Who knows us?' You turn things around!" (Isa. 29:13,15-16)

> When you cry out, let your collection of idols deliver you. (Isa. 57:13)

Their unfaithfulness was not hidden from the eyes of God. And it was through His servant Isaiah that the Faithful King revealed how he would bring the nation back into repentance. God would strip the nation of its splendor and let it fall into the hands of its enemies. He would allow calamity to overcome them and completely humiliate them. This was not a revengeful fit, but acting on the terms He had promised from the nation's birth.

> Then you will call, and the Lord will answer; you will cry, and He will say, "Here I am." If you remove the yoke from your midst... then your light will rise in darkness and your gloom will become like midday. (Isa. 58:9-10)

> Behold, I have refined you, but not as silver; I have tested you in the

> furnace of affliction. For My own sake, for My own sake, I will act; for how can My name be profaned? And My glory I will not give to another. (Isa. 48:10-11)

For those who would listen, He would redeem. The words of Isaiah emanated with God's redemption. Beautiful and tragic poetic discourses declared the coming Messiah. Many scoffed. Others took note and passed them on from generation to generation to seek the One who would save. Centuries after this prophet, Jesus would stand within the synagogue and open to the book of Isaiah and read the prophecy of Himself.

> And the book of Isaiah was handed to [Jesus]. And He opened the book and found the place where it was written, "The Spirit of the Lord is upon Me, because He anointed Me to preach the gospel to the poor. He has sent Me to proclaim release to the captives..." He closed the book, gave it back to the attendant and sat down; and the eyes of all in the synagogue were fixed on Him. And He began to say to them, "Today this Scripture has been fulfilled in your hearing." (Luke 4:17-21)

EXPERIENCE

In your kitchen, find three items that are good and satisfying to eat and three items that might taste or smell good but lack nutritional benefit. Explain the contrasts between the two groups. If you have ever grown hungry, or sick, or worked to exhaustion, which of these foods does your body crave? Which does it need?

When we go through times of trial or discipline, our true needs are often easily identified. Our hearts crave what is right and good. It is the purpose of discipline – to define and refine. The Lord disciplines His children so we will understand He is our only true Sustenance and Source of life.

> Every one who thirsts, come to the waters; and you who have no money come, buy and eat. Come, buy wine and milk without money and without cost. Why do you spend money for what is not bread, and your wages for what does not satisfy? Listen carefully to Me, and eat what is good, and delight yourself in abundance. Incline your ear and come to Me. Listen, that you may live. (Isa. 55:1-3)

May you have a heart of wisdom, a *hearing heart*, pursuing only that which is life-giving!

Read Isaiah 5:20 and pray concerning the ways you may have fed yourself with what was not satisfying.

DECEMBER 17

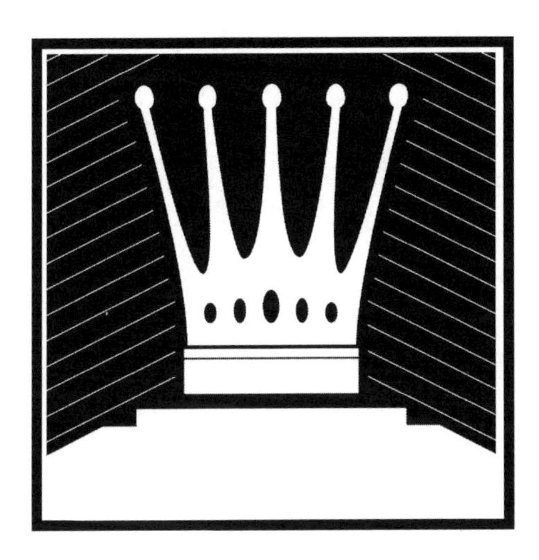

Good Kings

[If] My people who are called by My name humble themselves and pray and seek My face and turn from their wicked ways, then I will hear from heaven, will forgive their sin and will heal their land. Now My eyes will be open and My ears attentive to the prayer offered in this place (the temple)... As for you (Solomon), if you walk before Me as your father David walked, even to do according to all that I have commanded you, and will keep My statutes and My ordinances, then I will establish your royal throne as I covenanted with your father David, saying, "You shall not lack a man to be ruler in Israel." But if you turn away and forsake My statutes... then I will uproot you from My land which I have given you, and this house which I have consecrated for My name I will cast out of My sight and I will make it a proverb and a byword among all peoples.

2 Chronicles 7:14-20

The Lord was never vague about His promises to His people. He had crystal clear words for both the people of Israel and the kings who led them. But only a minority heeded His message. Those few, however, continued to pull God's word from the heap of dust, rubble, and desolation and remind the people of the One who had established them and could sustain them.

As you read through the books of Kings and Chronicles, it is recorded which kings followed God and which turned their backs on him. None were perfect, but their true allegiances became evident during their times of rule. The good kings applied God's words, trusting that what He had promised long before their generation was still binding in the days they lived. They believed God had the power to redeem an unfaithful people because *He* was faithful. The evil kings regarded His word as outdated, equal to or lesser than the gods of the neighboring nations, and lacking in comparison to their own wisdom.

King Asa "did good and right in the sight of the Lord his God, for he removed the foreign altars and high places, tore down the sacred pillars, cut down the Asherim, and commanded Judah to seek the Lord God of their fathers and to observe the law and the commandment" (2 Chron. 14:2-4). Jehoshaphat, his son, succeeded him as king and in like manner "his heart was courageous in the ways of the Lord."[1] Both kings had their faith tested on the battlefront. Both saw the odds of victory from man's standpoint as impossible, and both trusted that if God was with them then the victory was theirs. God blessed their courageous faith with strength and protection against their enemies.

Unfortunately, when King Ahaz ascended to the throne, his evil ways were despicable and utterly rebellious to the Lord. He sacrificed his sons to pagan gods. But amidst all this rebelliousness was one son who survived his father: Hezekiah. Imagine what it must have been like to be raised by a father whose evil actions were unpredictable and who had killed your siblings. We would likely dismiss any hope of goodness coming from this dangerous and dysfunctional family. But God's hand

1 2 Chron. 17:6 ESV

rested on this prince - a light in the darkness.

Hezekiah brought great reform to Judah. When he became king after his father's death, Hezekiah "opened the house of the Lord."[2] Immediately he gathered the priests and the Levites and ordered them to remove the pagan altars and cast them into the Kidron Valley. He instructed them to cleanse the temple completely and to consecrate it. Once the temple was purified, the people sang the songs of David.[3] Can you hear their voices? Loud and strong. Heads lifted to heaven, praising Him for all His immutable attributes. Bodies prostrate before Him, begging for His forgiveness.

Hezekiah reinstated the Passover celebration, and though it was not performed to strict protocol, God poured His blessing on them for their hearts were contrite. They were reminded of God's deliverance from their history and His promise for their future. What a celebration as it reoriented their focus on the true King and Deliverer!

The people experienced great peace during Hezekiah's reign. When Assyria threatened to overthrow and surround their fortified cities, and victory seemed bleak, Hezekiah gathered his military officers together.

> Be strong and courageous, do not fear or be dismayed because of the king of Assyria nor because of all the horde that is with him; for the one with us is greater than the one with him. With him is only an arm of flesh, but with us is the Lord our God to help us and to fight our battles. (2 Chron. 32:7-8)

On the battlefield with men waiting his command, Hezekiah urges them on under the banner of his Mighty King. And God mightily defended His people for His own sake.[4] Even on his deathbed with sickness depleting his body, Hezekiah cries out to the Merciful One.[5] His anointed position was more than a means for personal fame, but a platform for making the Lord's name great "that all the kingdoms of

---

2 2 Chron. 29:3
3 2 Chron. 29:27-29
4 2 Kings 19:32-36
5 Isa. 38:5

the earth may know."[6]

Unfortunately, Hezekiah's son and grandson chose to return to the ways of Ahaz, with evil and pagan acts. They rebuilt what the God-fearing Hezekiah had previously torn down. The temple was again desecrated, and the people, in the procession of their leaders, pursued wickedness. It is sobering to see what can transpire between two generations.

Then Josiah become ruler of this rogue nation. Where Hezekiah led in the *greatest* reform and revival of the people, Josiah led in the most *thorough* reform. He assumed reign at the age of eight. Incredibly at age 16, he began to purify the nation and seek the God of David. The Lord placed on the throne one who would not compromise. "He did not turn aside to the right or to the left" (2 Chron. 34:2 ESV). He didn't just throw the pagan altars and high places into the Kidron Valley. He chopped them up, grinded them down, and burned them. When Josiah was 26 years old, a priest found the book of the law the Lord had given to Moses and brought it to him.[7]

> And Shaphan read from it in the presence of the king. When the king heard the words of the law, he tore his clothes... [Then Josiah] read in their hearing all the words of the book of the covenant which was found in the house of the Lord. Then the king stood in his place and made a covenant before the Lord to walk after the Lord, and to keep His commandments and His testimonies and His statutes with all his heart and with all his soul, to perform the words of the covenant written in this book. (2 Chron. 34:18-19, 30-31)

Josiah moved the nation to once again observe the Passover in its fullness, in total reverence to the God they had so scorned. His leadership was rooted in his own commitment as he humbled himself to the *true* King, and pulled God's word from the heap to declare its constant and enduring truth.

---

6 2 Kings 19:19
7 Some scholars believe this refers to the book of Deuteronomy; others think it is the full Pentateuch.

EXPERIENCE

Use building blocks to see how high each person can build a tower without it falling over. Leave it standing.

The term "high place" is used repeatedly in the chronicles of the kings and nations of Judah and Israel. The evil kings allowed them and built them. The good kings tore them down and prohibited them. *High places* were literally high places of worship that were patterned after the worship practices of the surrounding pagan nations. They were built to be idols or altars for pagan gods and at times were even designated for God-worship. Even if this wasn't the intent, it was man's way of saying, "I will worship God on *my* terms," which of course is no reverence to God at all. Disregarding God's supremacy and holiness ended up being a snare to His people.

Asa and Jehosaphat removed the high places in certain areas, but failed to do so completely throughout the nation.[8] However, when Hezekiah and Josiah took the throne, their first order of business was to utterly destroy those places. It must have been quite apparent that these high places were a stumbling block to pure allegiance to the One True God.

Now have the youngest person knock down the high tower you built earlier.

Are there ways we tweak God's commands in order to make our lives more convenient or acceptable in our culture? Are there things in our lives we know God wants us to "utterly destroy" but we've allowed them to remain because we don't feel it causes too much damage? God does not change. His words and instructions are for our good. Will we trust Him?

Read how and why God's people are to purify themselves in Ephesians 5:6-17.

---

8 2 Chron. 15:17, 20:33

DECEMBER 18

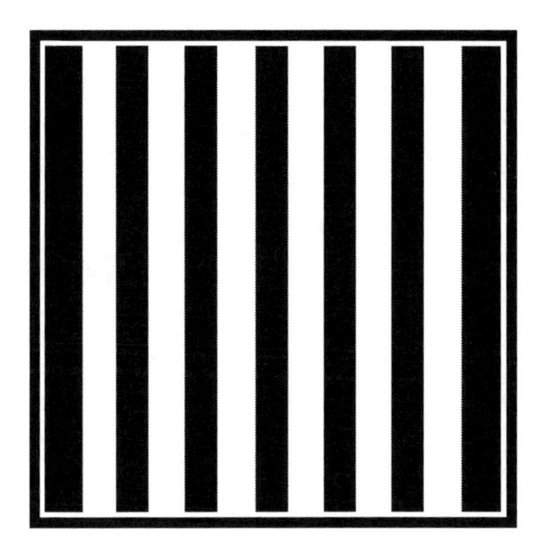

Captivity

Thus says the Lord of hosts, "Because you have not obeyed My words, behold...I will send to Nebuchadnezzar king of Babylon, My servant, and will bring them against this land and against its inhabitants and against all these nations round about; and I will utterly destroy them and make them a horror and a hissing, and an everlasting desolation... and these nations will serve the king of Babylon seventy years.
Jeremiah 25:8-12

I received a call this morning from my sister who just experienced one of the most bizarre and frightening accidents while driving to work that I've ever heard. While traveling in the far left lane on a highway bridge, she noticed the car in front of her swerve into the next lane. It was early morning, still dark, but she could see there was something in her lane. However, now trapped between a concrete median on her left, an 18-wheeler on her right, a car right behind her, and no time to brake, she hit the "thing" head-on, resulting in an explosion of fiberglass. When she finally pulled over and called the police, she discovered she had actually hit a bathtub that had just been reported as seen on the highway moments before. Thankfully, her car was the only casualty, but she was left speechless and shaken up. Who prepares to face a bathtub while driving to work?

As we recount the journey of Judah and Israel, we get a bird's eye view of where it is all headed. But for the nations involved, they had more of a bathtub-in-the-lane experience. With Egypt on one side and Babylon on the other, they slammed into an unimaginable obstacle. The faithful Josiah was killed unexpectedly, and his son, Jehoahaz, took over. Jehoahaz was wicked in the eyes of the Lord and found himself in bondage to Egypt.[1] Seems we've heard this story before.

Jehoiakim, his brother, was appointed king of Judah by the king of Egypt. But not long into his quasi-reign, he was bound in bronze chains and led away as a captive of Nebuchadnezzar, the king of Babylon. The first of three sieges on Jerusalem began. The temple articles were pillaged, making a strong statement that control had been handed over. Judah lost its pride and name.[2] Jehoiakim's son, Jehoiachin, was also evil, but he only lasted three months before Nebuchadnezzar added him to Babylon's treasures. The foreign king then appointed Zedekiah as the new king of Judah, but he too continued in the footsteps of the prideful kings and rebelled against both God and Nebuchadnezzar. In this final siege, the temple was burned, Jerusalem was destroyed to its foundations, and God's people were exiled in Babylon.[3]

With the temple gone, where was the Lord? If they cried out, would He even be there to hear? Would He care? These descendants of Abraham, the receivers of the covenant, were left speechless. As they processed this situation, they surely must have recalled the words of the prophets foretelling the pending discipline of God. They probably wondered if they had *missed* the Deliverer coming from the line of

---

1 2 Kings 23:29-34
2 2 Kings 23:34-24:5
3 2 Kings 24:6-25:11

David or worse – that God was no longer intending to send Him.

Now they were exiled to another nation, one that did not claim God as the One True God. A foreign king had taken their temple articles and put them into his own pagan temples. But God was not silent during this time. He sent Jeremiah and other prophets to speak His message to a faithful minority, the *remnant.* They would have ears to hear.

> Now these are the words of the letter which Jeremiah the prophet sent…"Thus says the Lord of hosts, the God of Israel, to all the exiles whom I have sent into exile from Jerusalem to Babylon, 'Build houses and live in them; and plant gardens and eat their produce. Take wives and become the fathers of sons and daughters, and take wives for your sons and give your daughters to husbands, that they may bear sons and daughters; and multiply there and do not decrease. Seek the welfare of the city where I have sent you into exile, and pray to the Lord on its behalf; for in its welfare you will have welfare.'…For thus says the Lord, 'When seventy years have been completed for Babylon, I will visit you and fulfill My good word to you, to bring you back to this place. For I know the plans that I have for you,' declares the Lord, 'plans for welfare and not for calamity to give you a future and a hope. Then you will call upon Me and come and pray to Me, and I will listen to you. You will seek Me and find Me when you search for Me with all your heart.'"
> (Jer. 29:1-13)

Purpose in exile. Light in darkness. Notice how many times God referred to *His* doing in all that had taken place: "the exiles *I* have sent into exile"… "where *I* have sent you"… "*I* will visit you and fulfill"… "*I* know the plans *I* have"… "*I* will listen."

One of the remnant, Daniel, heard these words. Hananiah, Mishael, and Azariah (better known by their Babylonian names Shadrach, Meshach, and Abednego) heard these words. Ezekiel heard these words. Mordecai heard these words. All were living in those volatile times, yet *they* remained steadfast. God's faithful remnant worked within the land, merged with the people, honored the government, but kept allegiance to their God. They bore the weight of God's discipline, but they lived obediently, anticipating their time to return, hoping in God's blessing and the renewal of His people.

Adjusting under threatening leadership, Daniel and his friends sought God's unique direction day-to-day, even as they were confronted with opportunities of compromise and faced the displeasure of the kingdom for not complying to pagan ways. When Shadrach, Meshach and Abednego faced a fiery furnace because they would not worship Nebuchadnezzar's golden image, their resilient confidence in the Lord bolstered them to stand fast in obedience.

> O Nebuchadnezzar... our God whom we serve is able to deliver us from the furnace of blazing fire; and He will deliver us out of your hand, O king. But even if He does not, let it be known to you, O king, that we are not going to serve your gods or worship the golden image that you have set up. (Dan. 3:16-18)

This is, after all, what God had asked of His people from the very beginning – to serve Him with all their heart, soul, and might.[4] God chose Israel as His servant. This nation was to be a light to *all* the nations, bringing the good news of salvation to *all* the earth, to kings and to countries, to the forsaken and the lost.[5] How remarkable that it was in captivity many would come to see their God in His greatest splendor.

EXPERIENCE

Sketch a simple drawing and show it to everyone else. Give a few minutes for each person to draw on their own piece of paper as close a representation as they can by viewing your example.

---

4 Deut. 6:1-5
5 Isa. 49

Now, draw another simple picture, but don't allow the others to see it. Using only verbal instructions, explain how to draw it while others attempt to replicate it on their own paper. Share your drawings.

What kind of instructions did you have to give? How was the second task more difficult than the first?

In the first drawing task, you looked at the drawing whenever you felt it was needed. When you finished drawing, you stopped looking. This is much like God's people. In the beginning they lived in the liberty of communing with God and knowing His law whenever they wished. Eventually it seemed unnecessary to keep looking up and instead it felt like rote procedure.

In the second drawing task, your success rested solely on your willingness to hear, follow, and have instructions repeated. You didn't know the task was over until the originator said you were done. It required your attention and obedience. In exile, God's people found themselves in a very similar place. Captivity required their contrite attention and under these unfavorable circumstances the Lord taught His children to walk again, trust His timing, and remember His promise to redeem.

Read Daniel's prayerful confession in Daniel 9:1-19. Can you agree with David in Psalm 119:67,71?

DECEMBER 19

Zerubbabel

O Lord, in accordance with all Your righteous acts, let now Your anger and Your wrath turn away from Your city Jerusalem, Your holy mountain; for because of our sins and the iniquities of our fathers, Jerusalem and Your people have become a reproach to all those around us...O my God, incline Your ear and hear! Open Your eyes and see our desolations and the city which is called by Your name; for we are not presenting our supplications before You on account of any merits of our own, but on account of Your great compassion. O Lord hear! O Lord, forgive! O Lord, listen and take action! For Your own sake, O my God, do not delay, because Your city and Your people are called by Your name.
Daniel 9:16-19

Daniel's appeal to the Lord was made 67 years after he was taken into Babylonian captivity. He had memorized the words of Jeremiah who prophesied that the rebuilding of Jerusalem would take place after

70 years of bondage. For all those years, Daniel clung to the promise of the Lord, until finally, King Cyrus of Persia allowed the Israelites to return to the desolated Jerusalem.

> The Lord stirred up the spirit of Cyrus, king of Persia, so that he sent a proclamation throughout all his kingdom, and also put it in writing, saying… "The Lord, the God of heaven, has given me all the kingdoms of the earth and He has appointed me to build Him a house in Jerusalem, which is in Judah. Whoever there is among you of all His people, may his God be with him! Let him go up to Jerusalem which is in Judah and rebuild the house of the Lord, the God of Israel; He is the God who is in Jerusalem." (Ezra 1:1-3)

King Cyrus equipped nearly 50,000 Jews with substantial means by which to rebuild Jerusalem: building materials, money, and even the temple articles that Nebuchadnezzar had taken. Led by Zerubbabel (the governor of Judah) and Joshua (the high priest), the people rebuilt the altar of the Lord on its foundation, began offering sacrifices again, and even celebrated the Feast of Tabernacles.

Zerubbabel was a key figure during this season of rebuilding. Much of the book of Haggai contains God's words to him. In the New Testament, Matthew records the lineage of Christ from Abraham to Joseph. Right in the middle of this Messianic line we will discover a crack in the branch that has been restored. "After the deportation to Babylon, Jeconiah (King Jehoiachin) became the father of Shealtiel, and Shealtiel the father of Zerubbabel" (Matt. 1:12). Going back several generations, remember that King Jehoiachin, Zerubbabel's grandfather, was one of the last evil kings to rule over Judah. It was during *his* reign that Nebuchadnezzar sent the people into exile. Jehoiachin was also cursed by God:

> "As I live," declares the Lord, "even though Jehoiachin… *were a signet ring on My right hand, yet I would pull you off*… Write this man down childless, a man who will not prosper in his days; for no man of his descendants will prosper sitting on the throne of David or ruling again in Judah." (Jer. 22:24-30)

The branch was broken by the hand of the Gardener.

Zerubbabel is the grandson of this king cursed by God. He was born in exile, a result of the disobedience of God's chosen people. "Zerubbabel" means *seed of Babylon.* Surely, his name was a reminder of the curse.[1] And now Zerubbabel was commanded to rebuild Jerusalem.

For 17 years, he and the high priest worked at rebuilding the temple, but local opposition thwarted their progress. One day, the prophet Haggai arrived, bearing a prophetic message from God and a declaration to Zerubbabel, this "son of Babylon:"

> "I am going to shake the heavens and the earth. I will overthrow the thrones of kingdoms and destroy the power of the kingdoms of the nations... On that day," declares the Lord of hosts, "I will take you, Zerubbabel, son of Shealtiel, My servant," declares the Lord, "and *I will make you like a signet ring, for I have chosen you,*" declares the Lord of hosts. (Hag. 2:21-23)

What is God doing here? Zerubbabel, though a seemingly hidden branch of the Christmas tree, is worth our attention. We might see him as our brother, for what God performs on Zerubbabel's behalf is a portrayal of what He has done for us. According to Galatians 3 and 4, we *too* fall under a curse as a result of our rebellion. We have failed to keep His law, unable to do so by our own efforts. We are all *sons of Babylon.* "The wages of sin is death" and "all have sinned."[2] Our own sin breaks us and cuts off our line to the Divine; the signet ring has been pulled off. But "when the fullness of time came, God sent forth His Son, born of a woman, born under the Law, so that He

---

1 To his correct lineage, there is some controversy for many accounts in Scripture list him as the direct descendant of Jehoiachin through Shealtiel (Matt. 1:12, Ezra 3:2; Neh. 12:1, Hag. 1:1), while the Chronicles' record records Shealtiel as Zerubbabel's uncle (1 Chron. 3:15-19). Though this may seem like an insignificant detail, the kingly line was tremendously important to the promise of God. Remember they were looking for a King to come through the line of David.

To this seemingly conflicting detail, it has been suggested that possibly Shealtiel died early and his brother Pedaiah married his widow and raised his son Zerubbabel, making him the rightful heir. Others have suggested that this is how the curse does not extend to Zerubbabel. Regardless, Zerubbabel, this son of Babylon, is the legal successor of Shealtiel.

2 Rom. 3:23; 6:23

might redeem those who were under the Law, that we might receive *the adoption as sons*!" (Gal. 4:4-5). The curse is removed by *His* work, and He justly declares righteous those who believe. By His great grace, God has made us like His signet ring, adopted sons and daughters to the King.[3]

As a result of God's proclamation, Zerubbabel recommenced the temple work and completed it in just four years. About 68 years later Ezra, who was a high priest descendant of Aaron, set his heart on leading the people back to God and His Word.[4] He also received permission from the reigning Artaxerxes (several kings since Cyrus) to rebuild the city of Jerusalem and the hearts of its people. Fourteen years from Ezra's return, God moved in the heart of the king's cupbearer, Nehemiah, who served in Persia's capital Susa. God's hand was upon him as he approached the king to request permission to return to Jerusalem to rebuild its walls. His request was granted.[5] Like Zerubbabel, Nehemiah faced opposition when he returned, but he faithfully led the people and rebuilt the wall in less than two months.

Perhaps the city name Susa rings a bell? It was the setting of the events in the book of Esther that took place about 40 years earlier. Remember God's provision as Esther gained the favor of King Xerxes and through wise counsel responded boldly to stop a pending genocide of the Jews? God continued to preserve His people, ensuring the growth of a tree, which bore His name.

So, at this point I ask you to take a few steps back from this mended branch to see the nurturing of the tree. Close up, with all the new growth here and there, the eyesore of a hemorrhaged trunk, and cumbersome needles masking its beauty, it can seem like a disconnected mess. Sure you can identify branches of hope, but with God's chosen people scattered everywhere and not in the land of promise, could God still be in control? It may seem like His plan is at best crippled, barely maintaining a semblance of what He promised. But the Lord has no plan to "fix" or recreate the tree. Instead, He faithfully nurtures because

---

3 2 Cor. 6:15-18
4 Ezra 7:10
5 Neh. 1:1-2:8

the Gardener has declared the end from the beginning.[6] From where we stand, can we declare that this Christmas tree is marvelous in our eyes?[7]

EXPERIENCE

Locate a room or particular part of the house that needs cleaning. Using a timer, give yourselves a designated amount of time, perhaps five or ten minutes, and see how much progress you can make.

Discuss the thought process behind each person's strategy in tackling the area. What part of the room did you clean first? How did you determine your strategy? What seemed priority and why? Did someone take a leadership role or did you all clean as you saw best?

When the people went to rebuild Jerusalem and its temple, they had varying ideas as to how and when it should be done. Therefore God appointed specific leaders to direct and encourage His people to accomplish the task.

Consider what each of these groups might have felt toward the rebuilding efforts:

- Those who had lived in Jerusalem at the time of its destruction or saw the temple being destroyed (older generation).
- Those who were born in exile, never knowing what Jerusalem was like before (younger generation).
- Mixed races who lived in and around the area and called it *home.*

Read Isaiah 44:24-28 and be comforted in knowing that the Lord is aware of every person and every circumstance in the midst of chaos.

6 Isa. 46:9-10
7 Ps. 118:16-24

DECEMBER 20

Prophecy

The people who walk in darkness will see a great light; those who live in a dark land, the light will shine on them.
Isaiah 9:2

Adam and Eve, ashamed and lost, listened closely to God's words as He cursed the serpent. They did not stand against Satan, nor could they make right what they had done. But God began telling the story of One who would crush the serpent. "I will put enmity between you (Satan) and the woman, and between your seed and her seed; He shall crush you on the head, and you shall bruise him on the heel" (Gen. 3:15).

The curse and blessing was repeated from generation to generation. God did not repeal it, for it was not contingent on the performance of man. It was contingent on His purpose alone. A promise of redemption was set into motion. It survived a great flood and sojourned with Abraham, even when he gazed on his son, the promised heir, laid out on the sacrificial altar. God confirmed to Abraham, "In your seed all the nations of the earth shall be blessed, because you have obeyed My voice" (Gen. 22:18).

His sure promise was spoken through the man Israel to his son Judah, with a broken past, drowning in consequences. It was a blessing characterized with kingship and sovereignty. The One who would crush would surely lead the nations. "The scepter shall not depart from Judah, nor the ruler's staff from between his feet, until Shiloh comes, and to him shall be the obedience of the peoples" (Gen. 49:10).

God's chosen people, His prized possession, demanded kings. God anointed a shepherd boy who would reign with His heart. Even this was not the final fulfillment, however, only a picture of the One who would save. Before David breathed his last breath, God further revealed His Chosen One. "When your days are complete and you lie down with your fathers, I will raise up your descendant after you, who will come forth from you... and I will establish the throne of his kingdom forever" (2 Sam. 7:12-13).

The effort to locate this King began in earnest. Volumes of kings' chronicles were searched, but none was found to fit the silhouette disclosed from the beginning. Any hope became a dim light, certainly nothing to separate the darkness. Micah whispered prophetically from a dark king's reign:

> But as for you, Bethlehem Ephrathah, too little to be among the clans of Judah, from you One will go forth for Me to be ruler in Israel. His goings forth are from long ago, from the days of eternity. (Mic. 5:2)

Isaiah heard the same tender voice and approached Satan's reigning vessel, King Ahaz, to declare how we would know the identity of the true King. "Therefore the Lord Himself will give you a sign: Behold, a virgin will be with child and bear a son, and she will call His name Immanuel" (Isa. 7:14).

Solomon, wise and honored beyond Judah's boundaries, saw a greater King to whom the nations and all wise men would bow down, their Crowns paying homage.

> Let the kings of Tarshish and the islands bring presents; the kings of Sheba and Seba offer gifts. And let all kings bow down before him, all nations serve him. (Ps. 72:10-11)

This redemption song would strum minor chords, as Hosea's life testified: "Out of *Egypt* I called My son" (Hosea 11:1). Victory would require tragedy and defeat. His royal carpet would be stained with blood from his first breath to his last. Satan's bruising on the heel would begin to appear, wound after wound. But Malachi was reassured that He would not stumble for another would clear His way.

> Behold, I am going to send My messenger, and he will clear the way before Me. And the Lord, whom you seek, will suddenly come to His temple; and the messenger of the covenant in whom you delight, behold, He is coming. (Mal. 3:1)

And though "the eyes of the blind will be opened and the ears of the deaf will be unstopped" by the coming of this Chosen One, it would be His claim to be greater than any earthly king that would catch their attention.[1] The Father would say to Him, "You are My Son, today I have begotten You" (Ps. 2:7).

The crowd would become silent before this King, God's Son. And as on the first day of Creation, when God separated light from darkness, the people would be divided in who they believed Him to be. Generations earlier, Isaiah had envisioned the scene as it would play out – loyalties failing and masses turning away. He lamented, "He was despised, and we did not esteem Him… We ourselves esteemed Him stricken, smitten of God, and afflicted" (Isa. 53:3-4). As Zechariah waved his hands in the air and pleaded with the people to turn back, he boldly declared, "Behold, your king is coming to you; He is just and endowed with salvation, humble, and mounted on a donkey, even on a colt, the foal of a donkey" (Zech. 9:9).

When the King would arrive, the Enemy would fight him

---

1 Isa. 35:5-6

ferociously, even poisoning those closest to His throne. The Son of God knew long before that "even my close friend in whom I trusted, who ate my bread, has lifted up his heel against me" for 30 pieces of silver.[2] This Chosen One of God, so long anticipated, would be falsely accused and hated "without cause".[3] And when this Shepherd King would be struck, His sheep would scatter and hope disappear.[4]

> All of us like sheep have gone astray, each of us has turned to his own way; but the Lord has caused the iniquity of us all to fall on Him. (Isa. 53:6)

Then darkness, O darkness; they knew it would come. The song would be silenced; the battle emerge as done.

> He was oppressed and he was afflicted, yet He did not open His mouth; like a lamb that is led to slaughter, and like a sheep that is silent before its shearers, so He did not open His mouth... He was taken away... His grave was assigned with wicked men, yet He was with a rich man in His death... But the Lord was pleased to crush Him, putting Him to grief; if He would render Himself as a guilt offering... [The Father] will see it and be satisfied... He Himself bore the sin of many, and interceded for the transgressors. (Isa. 53:7-12)

> My God, my God, why have You forsaken me?... A reproach of men and despised by the people. All who see me sneer at me; they mock me, they wag the head, saying, "Commit yourself to the Lord; let Him deliver him; let Him rescue him, because He delights in him"... I am poured out like water, and all of my bones are out of joint; my heart is like wax; it is melted within me. My strength is dried up like a potsherd, and my tongue cleaves to my jaws; and You lay me in the dust of death... A band of evildoers has encompassed me; they pierced my hands and my feet. I can count all my bones. They look, they stare at me; they divide my garments

2 Ps. 41:9, Zech. 11:12-13
3 Ps. 69:4
4 Zech. 13:7

> among them, and for my clothing they cast lots. (Ps. 22:1-18)

David cried out these prophetic words 1000 years before the Messiah appeared. It was a foretelling fulfilled, not by hopeful seekers, but by the very ones who wanted to discredit and eliminate Him. David foresaw a type of execution that was specifically Roman and centuries from anything to which David would have known or been exposed. God's watchmen were puzzled by David's words: How could the King reign if He was to die? How could an everlasting kingdom *fall*? But David sang in sweet refrain, "You will not allow Your Holy One to undergo decay" (Ps. 16:10).

This entire story was laid out centuries upon centuries before a star ever showed the way. His name, His position, His ministry, His death written so that we would *see* Him when He came.

> For a child will be born to us, a son will be given to us; and the government will rest on His shoulders; and His name will be called Wonderful Counselor, Mighty God, Eternal Father, Prince of Peace. (Isa. 9:6)

EXPERIENCE

Have each person think of a Christmas song. Choose someone to begin and hum the first note of the song. Stop and see if anyone can guess the name of the song from that one note. If not, then hum the first two notes and allow everyone to guess. Continue adding notes until someone guesses correctly. Allow people to reveal their song in this manner. As more and more notes are included, the song is no longer a mystery.

Consider how God's prophecy of the coming Messiah is a group of divinely chosen musicians, each with their instruments and voices, being strung together through time onto a stage. God places their parts on their stands. They've never seen the sheet music and are in the dark as to how their parts will blend with the others. They hold their instruments ready, eyes on their Conductor. The Ancient of Days lifts His hands; the audience is silent. Musicians take a breath...

What have we to say of this masterpiece, this grand opus? What have we to say of this Maestro?

Read Isaiah 52:13 - 53:12 and consider how Isaiah and his audience may have received this piece of the prophecy 700 years before Christ appeared.

DECEMBER 21

Silence

My soul, wait in silence for God only, for my hope is from Him.
Psalm 62:5

Silence is not always a welcome guest. It tends to fill voided spaces and find us in our devastated places. It permeates the air when we have nothing left to say or we've expended every answer. Silence brings discomfort when we want to hide behind noise or activity. Silence implies waiting. Waiting for answers, for direction, for understanding. The silence may be received reluctantly, but it often forces us to look beyond the immediate chaos. Silence, unlike any other experience, has the capacity to *correct* and *renew.*

In times of silence, we beg God to do something dramatic, don't we? *Let me know You are there!* But our pleas for a sign are typically based on how we *want* to see God. Elijah was a major prophet during the times of the kings who had experienced great manifestations of

God's presence. But when he didn't see revival and his ruthless enemies continued to threaten, Elijah hiked into the wilderness and declared to God, "It is enough... take my life" (1 Kings 19:4).

He retraced the steps Moses took to Mount Sinai, where the iconic leader had experienced God's presence and great outpourings of His power. Thunder. Earthquakes. Clouds. Shekinah glory. Perhaps God would grant Elijah the same glory. He stood on the mountain before the Lord,

> And a great and strong wind was rending the mountains and breaking in pieces the rocks before the Lord; but the Lord was not in the wind. And after the wind an earthquake, but the Lord was not in the earthquake. After the earthquake a fire, but the Lord was not in the fire; and after the fire a sound of a gentle blowing. When Elijah heard it, he wrapped his face in his mantle and went out and stood in the entrance of the cave. (1 Kings 19:11-13)

We don't want God to blow a gentle breeze, barely discernable enough see the hair rise and fall on our foreheads. We want the storm. The silence is unnerving. What exactly are we to *do*?

Israel's well-known history contained eras of prophecies, miracles, verbal conversations, and countless battles won by God's mighty hand. He created a flood, provided manna, shut the mouths of lions, and even sent fire down from heaven. Then, remarkably, after many exiled Jews began to return and rebuild, all of God's interaction with Israel seemed to come to a screeching halt. Silence filled the space. And God *allowed* it.

The scattered nation sought to find their purpose under a succession of foreign powers (just as Daniel had prophesied), first under Persian, then Egyptian, then Grecian rule, and finally subject to the oppressive power of Rome.[1] They called out but were met with only silence from the One who had originally blessed them. So their attention was directed to the written word – what He had already said. This would be their only lifeline. The prophecies of a Messiah

1 Dan. 2:26-47

were visited and revisited, discussed, and examined again. The people retraced the paths of their fathers, trying to make sense, trying to anticipate what God would do. But God blew only a gentle breeze. No fire, no thunder, no voice from heaven, no anointed messenger. He ordained the calendars to continue until His appointed day. He chose to make his people simply wait.

As they waited through calamitous days, many Jews cast aside the word of God as if it were nothing more than memories of a golden time, long past. For centuries, God spoke through His messengers: both prophets and priests, kings and judges. But the post exilic Jews resembled little like the former people of the promise. God's voice and revelation faded into a background of national transition and political defeat. Still, the Almighty One remained silent.

In the last book of the Old Testament, the prophet Malachi proclaimed God's final words to the scattered people in these silent days.

> "Your words have been arrogant against Me," says the Lord. "Yet you say, 'What have we spoken against You?'
>
> "You have said, 'It is vain to serve God; and what profit is it that we have kept His charge, and that we have walked in mourning before the Lord of hosts? So now we call the arrogant blessed; not only are the doers of wickedness built up but they also test God and escape.'"
>
> Then those who feared the Lord spoke to one another, and the Lord gave attention and heard it, and a book of remembrance was written before Him for those who fear the Lord and who esteem His name.
>
> "They will be Mine," says the Lord of hosts, "on the day that I prepare My own possession, and I will spare them as a man spares his own son who serves him."
>
> So you will again distinguish between the righteous and the wicked, between one who serves God and one who does not serve Him. (Mal. 3:13-18)

As the people allowed self-importance to obscure God's presence and scrutinized any measurable benefit of following Him, we find a remnant gathering together, encouraging one another, remembering what God had done, and trusting in His character. For these faithful few, God's silence, though uncomfortable, ignited a resiliency grounded in truth. The Israelite's response to God's silence highlighted those who trusted Him and who did not.

For 400 years God did not send out a new word of prophecy or instruction, yet the Christmas tree quietly extended and grew, bough after bough. So thick, its branches bore the likes of kings and expats, shepherds and slaves, and now just commonplace exiles trying to find their way. They could follow the branch somewhat. Line of Judah. Line of David. But after so many years they were going to need a sign of the coming Messiah who was to save. Would they recognize Him when He came?

> Therefore the Lord Himself will give you a sign: Behold, a virgin will be with child and bear a son, and she will call His name Immanuel. (Isa. 7:14)

> But as for you, Bethlehem Ephrathah, too little to be among the clans of Judah, from you One will go forth for Me to be ruler in Israel. His goings forth are from long ago, from the days of eternity. (Mic. 5:2)

EXPERIENCE

Turn off any background noise and sit in silence for a while. What new sounds do you hear? Make a list of the sounds you discover when you remove distractions.

When you don't see God moving or can't see His answer to a prayer, what might God want you to notice? What might He desire that you remember?

Sing together "O Come, O Come Emmanuel." Listen to the words that focus on waiting for the coming of the Lord in those years of silence.

Note *why* we can be still and wait on the Lord in Psalm 46.

DECEMBER 22

Zechariah

And you, child, will be called the prophet of the Most High; for you will go on before the Lord to prepare His ways; to give to His people the knowledge of salvation by the forgiveness of their sins.
Luke 1:76-77

The stage had been set. By the words of Daniel, given to him by the angel Gabriel, empires rose and fell just as God declared. Down to the year. The Jews lived beneath Rome's iron fist. Though they were not forced to adopt Rome's pagan central belief or recognize Caesar as their god, they paid for this "freedom" through exorbitant taxing. Herod the Great was their king as Judea was now a Roman province under his watch. As God's people looked around them, they saw evidence and reminders of a land that was long ago lost to their oppressors. They had fallen as a nation and had not experienced any new word from God Himself in over 400 years. They didn't see how

God was working behind the scenes, how he would again use the unexpected to accomplish his plan.

King Herod had rebuilt a great temple for the Jews out of self-inflation and to appease a historically problematic people. He also viciously forced his authority on the priests who would or would not serve within the land and in the Temple. The golden structure was symbolic of the state of the people: lackluster hearts overlaid with the influences of the culture. Spiritual sincerity turned into political advantage. Still, many held on to a sliver of pride as God's favored by submitting to rote obedience. And His remnant found their hope tested as they waited.

It is on this stage and before this backdrop where we are introduced to the priest Zechariah.[1]

Zechariah (or Zacharias) was a priest, probably one of approximately 18,000 priests who served in Israel at this time. He and his wife, Elizabeth, both came from the priestly line of Aaron. It was greatly honored to come from Aaron's line (the first high priest), and scripture describes Zechariah and Elizabeth as walking blamelessly before the Lord. Sadly, Zechariah and Elizabeth were past childbearing age and had no children to continue this heritage. Still, they continued to follow God who they considered sovereign and right.

When the time came, Zechariah left his hometown to perform his priestly duties in Jerusalem at the temple. This priestly organization was first inaugurated by King David, who divided the priests into 24 groups, named after the sons of Levi.[2] When the temple was destroyed and the people were taken into exile, these duties came to a halt and much of the priestly line was lost due to the scattering. However, when the exiles were allowed to return 70 years later, the people worked to retrace those family lines and reinstate the 24 priestly groups as best they could. In addition to keeping the three main Jewish feasts, each group was then assigned two weeks out of each year to serve in Jerusalem at the temple as detailed in Leviticus. Zechariah was from the Abijah division and

1 Luke 1:5
2 1 Chron. 23-24

it was his time to serve alongside hundreds of other priests from this same line.

Not all the priests could enter the temple's Holy Place and offer the prayers of the people to the Lord by way of incense. The priest who would perform this act was appointed by casting lots. It was the apex of their position to be chosen. Though many priests never received this privilege, on *this* occasion, the lot remarkably fell to Zechariah.[3]

He carried the bowl of ashes from the altar of the Lord into the Holy Place and there burned sweet incense. And though he was to be alone behind the curtain, to the right of this smoking altar stood an angel of the Lord. Zechariah trembled with fear.

> Do not be afraid, Zacharias, for your petition has been heard, and your wife Elizabeth will bear you a son, and you will give him the name John… he will be filled with the Holy Spirit while yet in his mother's womb. And he will turn many of the sons of Israel back to the Lord their God. It is he who will go as a forerunner before Him in the spirit and power of Elijah, to turn the hearts of the fathers back to the children, and the disobedient to the attitude of the righteous, so as to make ready a people prepared for the Lord. (Luke 1:13-17)

There is no doubt Zechariah recognized the angel's words as none other than the last words of prophecy from Malachi heard over 400 years before. "Behold, I am going to send you Elijah the prophet before the coming of the great and terrible day of the Lord. He will restore the hearts of the fathers to their children" (Mal. 4:5-6). Yet Zechariah was not sure how this news was meant for him, as his wife was well past childbearing age. He questioned the angel, "How will I know this for certain?"

How many times have we second-guessed how we could possibly do what God has called us to do? We hesitate in our marriages, as parents, in ministry, on our jobs, or when suffering. Recognizing our own limits can default us to view God's instruction as conditional or

---

3 Luke 1:8-9

generally implied. *If He only understood the uniqueness of my case,* right? But this is where God reminds us of His supremacy and ability. This is where He shines brightly.

Notice the angel's response. *"I am Gabriel, who stands in the presence of God."* Again, this significantly struck Zechariah's memory to recall when Gabriel last made his appearance in history. It was to Daniel when laying out the coming events concerning the exchange of ruling nations to come, all of which was fulfilled before and during the time of silence. God's word is sure. This same angel, who sees the face of God, was speaking God's word. There was no mistake.

Gabriel caused Zechariah to become mute until his promised son was born. *This* was his sign. Elizabeth became pregnant and surely walked in complete astonishment – her husband could no longer speak, and she was carrying a child who would make straight the path for the long-awaited Messiah. For nine months Zechariah and Elizabeth walked in faith, and then Elizabeth bore a son. On the day of circumcision, the people gathered and insisted that the child be named after his father, but Zechariah wrote down "*His name is John,*" and his lips were opened.[4]

Zechariah burst forth in praise, describing the Lord as a keeper of His word, His favor, and His anointing. This was *God's* work. As one who had memorized the prophecies in Scripture, Zechariah recognized the Lord as the Fulfiller of His promises.

> And you, child, will be called the prophet of the Most High; for you will go on before the Lord to prepare His ways; to give to His people the knowledge of salvation by the forgiveness of their sins, because of the tender mercy of our God, with which the Sunrise from on high will visit us, to shine upon those who sit in darkness and the shadow of death, to guide our feet into the way of peace. (Luke 1:76-79)

And though this child was born six months before Jesus, John the Baptizer would grow to make the claim, "He who comes after me has a higher rank than I, for *He existed before me*" (John 1:15).

---

4 Luke 1:59-64

EXPERIENCE

Ask everyone to demonstrate or share how they remember dates, tasks, appointments, or goal-setting steps. What happens when you fail to utilize these methods?

The name "Zechariah" means *Yahweh remembers.* What a fitting declaration. God *remembers.* Our use of the word remember typically signifies something brought to mind that was forgotten. However, the use of remember in Scripture most often referred to one's *response to a promise.* For example, in Genesis 8:1 when Noah and his family were confined within the ark during the flood, the Bible says, "But God remembered Noah... and God caused a wind to pass over the earth, and the water subsided." Also, when Moses fled to Midian, "God remembered His covenant with Abraham, Isaac, and Jacob."[5] The phrase does not insinuate a forgetful God who is in need of man to jog His memory. On the contrary, the phrase illustrates the I AM who is timely responding in covenant to His people. It is an active description expressing that because He is faithful to His word, He will act *now.*

Examine how the Lord reminded the people of His promises throughout history. Unlike God, why do we need reminding of His promises?

As you consider your battles, your circumstances, your unknown future, do not be tempted to view God as one who has forgotten His promises. His word is sure. *Yahweh remembers.* Instead be reminded of what He has said as true and trust that He will act on His word in His time and in His way.

Read Joshua 21:45 and 2 Peter 3:9.

---

5 Ex. 2:24

DECEMBER 23

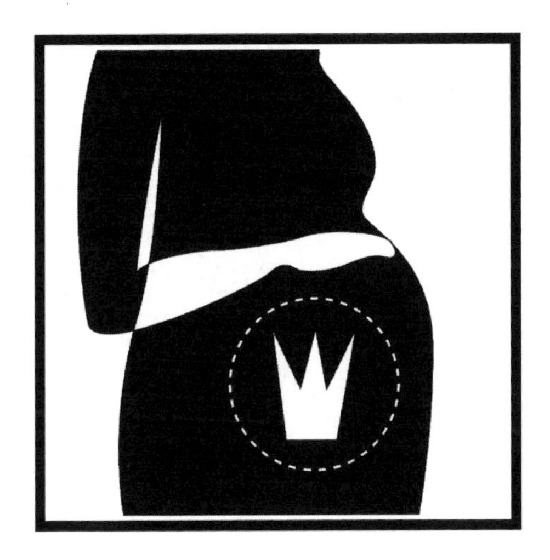

Mary

The angel said to her, "Do not be afraid, Mary; for you have found favor with God. And behold, you will conceive in your womb and bear a son, and you shall name Him Jesus. He will be great and will be called the Son of the Most High; and the Lord God will give Him the throne of His father David; and He will reign over the house of Jacob forever, and His kingdom will have no end."
Luke 1:30-33

I remember the day when the Scriptures I had known since childhood came alive. I could recite Bible stories and the *Roman Road*, had numerous Bible studies in my repertoire, and was armed with polished arguments on debatable Christian topics. I *did* believe and claimed to trust His Word, but honestly it all seemed a scattering of puzzle pieces. I worked to develop Christian disciplines, but they all appeared disjointed and wearisome. I struggled to maintain the goodness I had worked hard to achieve, but I could not see how all this worked in light of what I knew to be true. The Christian life seemed a heavy yoke.

Then one day, as I was working to *prove* myself to another believer, the God who I had been studying opened my eyes. As I read the same scriptures over and over, God picked up each of these seemingly unconnected truths and put the pieces together. I was broken at the misunderstanding I had made of all its parts. This God who I felt owed me was actually the One who poured His grace upon me when I was His enemy. For the first time I saw myself as one who truly needed a Savior. It seemed every verse was reintroducing me to my Lord I *thought* I knew. As I pondered it all, the Spirit worked, taking all the puzzle pieces of learned truths and fitting them together one by one – from the Law to His promises – giving me a more complete picture of who He was, is, and will forever be. I saw everything differently as God's grace took my eyes off me and fixed them on Him. My worldview exploded as I could see His dominion in every space.

Mary's response to the Lord choosing her among all women to be the mother of Jesus is absolutely fascinating. The angel, Gabriel, visited her with the personal announcement that she had been chosen to be the mother of the Messiah, "the Son of the Most High."[1] Out of honest confusion, she was unsure as to how this could take place as she had not yet *known* a man, though she was engaged to Joseph. Gabriel revealed that the Holy Spirit would come upon her, authenticating that Jesus would truly be the *Son of God.*

A million scenarios must have also overshadowed her at this point. This would be no ordinary birth, no ordinary family that could blend easily within the crowds of Nazareth. Instead, due to the incredulous circumstances of her pregnancy, she would be on display for fame or scorn. *Who could tell?* Gabriel addressed Mary's introspection by sharing the news concerning her close relative Elizabeth, assuring Mary that "nothing will be impossible with God."[2] Nothing.

Mary's response was not one of doubt or fear or inadequacy, but

1 Luke 1:31-33
2 Luke 1:36-37

she responded with strong faith in Yahweh, the God she had learned of all her life. "Behold, the bondslave of the Lord; may it be done to me according to your word" (Luke 1:38).

The "it" in this verse encompasses so many unknowns. When the angel described what kind of conception this would be, surely Mary considered what it meant. The Jewish law was clear on the punishment for an engaged woman who became pregnant outside of that covenant.[3] It was plausible that Joseph would not believe her and would abandon her. I'm sure she considered what the reaction would be from those in her family, friends, spiritual leaders, and the town as a whole. Humiliation. Misunderstanding. Persecution. Then, on top of all these possibilities, she was to raise a Messiah. *The Messiah.* Despite all the what-ifs, Mary trusted that if God ordained this, then He would sustain her. 'May *it* be done to me according to *Your* word."

Many have suggested Mary was chosen because of her obvious righteousness. I would beg to differ. Certainly she may have had strong faith; and by her own declaration, after seeing Elizabeth, we know she knew God's Word. But her words also disclose she in no way felt worthy of this blessed opportunity. Instead, she prominently magnified God's grace on her. He chose her out of His great pleasure, for His great purpose of loving and saving His own. In response, Mary's *Magnificat* confessed her position before the Lord.

> And Mary said, "My soul exalts the Lord, and my spirit has rejoiced in God my Savior." (Luke 1:46-47)

Despite what we may be prone to believe, Mary saw herself in need of saving. She did not see God as someone imploring her for a favor, but bestowing favor on one who *needed* a Savior.

> For He has had regard for the humble state of His bond slave; for behold, from this time on all generations will count me blessed. For the Mighty One has done great things for me; and holy is His name." (Luke 1:48-49)

3 Deut. 22:23-24

She was humbled He would choose *her* among all women. Mary recognized she would be called "blessed," though no one, not even she, could have dreamed this privilege would fall to her. If there had been a vote cast among all Judea, her name would not have made the ballot. Yet He loved her from the beginning, called her, and appointed her to carry the King. She couldn't respond in pride, for she was trembling in awareness of a sinful woman carrying the life of a perfect Messiah.

> And His mercy is upon generation after generation toward those who fear Him. He has done mighty deeds with His arm; He has scattered those who were proud in the thoughts of their heart. He has brought down rulers from their thrones, and has exalted those who were humble. He has filled the hungry with good things; and sent away the rich empty-handed. He has given help to Israel His servant, in remembrance of His mercy, as He spoke to our fathers, to Abraham and his descendants forever. (Luke 1:50-55)

At first glance this section of her response may seem a bit unrelated to the announcement. She talks about the proud, rulers and thrones, the hungry, and even Abraham. But in similar fashion, when the Holy Spirit began piecing everything I had known into a beautiful picture of God in truth, Mary took a step back and judged all things in light of God's character. It's as if everything she had known, questioned, wondered, and learned was now making marvelous sense. Her worldview was oriented to perceive that the same gracious work He was doing in her was only reflective of the same consistent work He was doing in the lives of all His people.

Mary's perspective is forever changed. From the birth of Jesus to His crucifixion, from seeing Him in the garden to the day of Pentecost, Mary would treasure "all these things, pondering them in her heart" (Luke 2:19).

EXPERIENCE

Name some of your favorite books or movies.

How many of these stories are "underdog" stories, where the one least likely to succeed finds victory? Why do we love these types of stories so much? Our heart cheers for the overlooked, despised, and humble character when we see him or her go against the world's odds.

Our lives reflect the same story line if we belong to the Lord. He gives hope to sinful people, rest for those who are weary, grace on those who don't deserve, and a glorious inheritance for those who are poor and empty. Because He took our sin and punishment upon His own shoulders and conquered death on our behalf, we can declare like Job, "The helpless has hope!" (Job 5:16).

Praise God for *how* and *why* He works in your life as you read 1 Corinthians 1:26-31.

DECEMBER 24

Joseph, the Husband of Mary

And Joseph her husband, being a righteous man and not wanting to disgrace her, planned to send her away secretly. But when he had considered this, behold, an angel of the Lord appeared to him in a dream, saying, "Joseph, son of David, do not be afraid to take Mary as your wife; for the Child who has been conceived in her is of the Holy Spirit. She will bear a Son; and you shall call His name Jesus, for He will save His people from their sins."
Matthew 1:19-21

On May 27, 1997 about mid-afternoon, one of the most dangerous, deadly tornados made its way through Jarrell, Texas. It's size and severity developed quickly and took the people in that area by surprise. State patrol expediently worked to shut off Interstate 35, in both directions, anticipating this 3/4-mile-wide tornado would eventually cross the interstate as it flirted along the edge of this major thoroughfare.

I had left home earlier that day, clear skies all around, to make my way up a 120-mile stretch of I-35. It was only four days before my wedding, and my fiancé was waiting for my arrival so we could secure our marriage license. I was full of joy and anticipation of what was to come later that week.

About an hour into my trip, a sprinkle of rain on my windshield developed into a blinding downpour. I was comfortable driving in Texas' thunderstorms, but this day I was nervous and eventually came to a complete stop with the other traffic on the interstate. The wind and rain blanketed my windshield in an opaque white. I began praying over and over, "Lord, please keep me safe." I searched the radio to find weather reports, all of which issued a barrage of warnings, "Take immediate cover... Tornados spotted near Jarrell... alongside I-35." I scanned my immediate surroundings for a ditch or an overpass and inched my way to the median, across the grass, and onto an access road. I heard an 18-wheeler blast his horn, but I could not see him.

Terrified, I found refuge in the parking lot of a gas station and ran inside to find the building packed with other stranded drivers. I asked them for details on the storm, but they all seemed just as lost. At one point, the station cashier stepped on top of the counter and hollered for everyone's attention. "The phones are not working and there are tornados nearby. I would suggest that everyone get their house in order!" I was numb. I felt as though days from my wedding I was having that blessing snatched from me.

After a tense period of time, the rain and wind died down to a quiet steady stream. We all returned to our cars and headed back to the highway, oblivious to the extent of destruction the tornado had delivered less than a mile away. I had been obliged to submit to something utterly out of my control, something that made me fear I'd lose everything I had long waited for.

Joseph, we could say, encountered a similar storm in his journey toward "until death do we part." Engaged, legally married and covenanted with Mary, Joseph had righteously planned out their future.

A carpenter by trade, he was making a way for them in Nazareth and certainly planned to one day fill their modest home in this town with little *Josephs* and *Marys* running around. However, a day came when a catastrophic *tornado* of sorts hit his well-ordered life. His betrothed was pregnant.

Imagine him wrestling in what to believe as Mary relayed her account of the angel's visit. "An angel appeared... Jesus... Son of God... favor with God... you will conceive."[1] Joseph trusted her, and he loved her, but we can surely empathize with him as he absorbed this news. How could he find himself in the middle of this storm on all sides? Suddenly he couldn't see a thing. His plans were obscured. He didn't know what the right thing to do was or the right way to go. So out of fear he *inched* his way across the median of his plans to take the best possible route by his estimation: divorce her secretly and keep their honor.

> But when he had considered this, behold, an angel of the Lord appeared to him in a dream, saying, "Joseph, son of David, do not be afraid to take Mary as your wife; for the Child who has been conceived in her is of the Holy Spirit. She will bear a Son; and you shall call His name Jesus, for He will save His people from their sins." (Matt. 1:20-21)

God's intent of getting his house in order was quite different than what Joseph had prepared. His fiancé Mary was the one Isaiah had prophesied about saying, "A virgin will be with child and bear a son, and she will call His name Immanuel" (Isa. 7:14). And though his future now seemed quite unpredictable, Joseph got up from his sleep, returned to the road, and took Mary as his wife. In obedience, Joseph trusted that God would direct that whirling wind of circumstantial fear and every contingency and cover them with His strong arm. He didn't have to know *how*, he just needed to *obey*.

So, the wedding remained on the calendar, but their anticipation took a sobering and precarious turn. On top of all that Joseph faced

1 Luke 1:26-35

as the protecting head of this union, he faced another logistical, but significant demand. At the time, Caesar Augustus was the reigning emperor of the Roman world. It was a common practice to take a census of the people within the occupied world, mainly for tax purposes. Caesar's mandate required Joseph to return to the city of his family line, which was Bethlehem, the city of David.[2] The timing of this census was not accidental. Again we find another decree, instated by a leader who knew little to nothing of God's prophecy, moving people to fulfill what Micah had prophesied centuries before.

> But as for you, Bethlehem Ephrathah, too little to be among the clans of Judah, from you One will go forth for Me to be ruler in Israel. His goings forth are from long ago, from the days of eternity. (Mic. 5:2)

So now in the midst of setting up home in Nazareth, a major road trip was required, one that probably seemed more of a nuisance for these soon-to-be parents than an act of God's hand. Yet, it was highly significant from His view. God kept His word, even that which we do not see.

Joseph, this carpenter, knew what it meant to see a beautiful finished product when viewing rough cut lumber. He knew the vision, the expert planning, the skillful handling, the required pressure, the cutting, and the craftsmanship to bring a work to its completion. Most who viewed the work in process were unable to envision what it would become. But not the carpenter. And how many times as Joseph labored over his work was he reminded of the God who declared what would be centuries beforehand? How many times would he appreciate God's fine workmanship to accomplish the task? For the coming Promised One, the boy whom he would soon hold, part of God's handiwork included him and his leadership of this chosen family. He was chosen to be the earthly father of the Son of God.

---

2 Luke 2:1-5

EXPERIENCE

Look at an inkblot or a silhouette. Ask everyone to share what they each see. Take note that most of the responses typically have to do with what you see in the darker portion of the whole frame. Not many people will focus on the white background to see what that form entails.

We tend to seek answers in the circumstances themselves and everything that those silhouettes encompass. But God is light. Do we consider how the white part of the canvas actually forms the silhouette? How can you stand back to see God working around and through you? Don't limit your idea of God's will by the circumstances and patterns alone. Trust His work in the background. He holds the full picture.

What can we trust in our distress? Read Psalm 118:5-9 and 1 Peter 4:19.

DECEMBER 25

Jesus

In the same region there were some shepherds staying out in the fields and keeping watch over their flock by night. And an angel of the Lord suddenly stood before them, and the glory of the Lord shone around them; and they were terribly frightened. But the angel said to them, "Do not be afraid; for behold, I bring you good news of great joy which will be for all the people; for today in the city of David there has been born for you a Savior, who is Christ the Lord."
Luke 2:8-11

The world in darkness waits to hear the herald of a king, a Messiah. Who will save? Felt within and beyond the Judean community was a hunger for one who would give them hope, victory, and establish a name above all names, a kingdom to reign the nations. From where would this good news come?

It is 9 BC and a Roman inscription has been carved into stone to celebrate the birth of Caesar Augustus. It reads, "Augustus… filled with virtue that he might benefit humankind, sending him as a savior, both for us and for our descendants... since the birthday of the god Augustus was the beginning of the good tidings for the world that came by reason of him..."[1] The nations fashioned their own god of salvation, propaganda requiring worship to one who they hoped, fingers crossed, would bring prosperity.

> Why are the nations in an uproar and the peoples devising a vain thing? The kings of the earth take their stand and the rulers take counsel together against the Lord and against His Anointed, saying, "Let us tear their fetters apart and cast away their cords from us!" He who sits in the heavens laughs, the Lord scoffs at them. Then He will speak to them in His anger and terrify them in His fury, saying, "But as for Me, I have installed My King upon Zion, My holy mountain." (Ps. 2:1-6)

No man would take God's kingdom. "I am the Lord, that is My name," He declares, "I will not give My glory to another" (Isa. 42:8). The time had come. He rallied His army of heavenly hosts. He sent Gabriel to set the stage. He moved the pen of the Roman leaders to decree a census, and He closed the doors of every crowded inn in Bethlehem.

The world in solemn stillness lay. Shepherds retired on a dark field, taking turns watching over black fields spotted white with wool. They scanned the plains for enemies, never suspecting to encounter the Shepherd's presence. Suddenly, the angel of the Lord stood before them, piercing the darkness, causing them to tremble in fear.

This brilliant angel heralded a message declaring "good news of great joy for all the people... a Savior, who is Christ the Lord!"[2] It is not a man-made fabrication of empty hope, but a fulfillment of truth that had been memorized since sin's first curse in the garden, and it was now inscribed on the hearts of those who believed.

---

1 The *Priene Calendar Inscription*, dated 9BC, heralds the good news ("gospel") of a new era within the Roman Empire at the birthday of Caesar Augustus.

2 Luke 2:8-16

As the angel gave the sign, "You will find a baby wrapped in cloths and lying in a manger," the sky was filled with the heavenly hosts, singing a song of redemption, "Glory to God in the highest, and on earth peace among men with whom He is pleased." Their presence declared Immanuel, *God with us!*

This is the Lord's perfect response to the world. This is His answer. The Psalmist says,

> I will surely tell of the decree of the Lord:
>
> [The Father] said to Me, "*You are My Son, today I have begotten You.* Ask of Me, and I will surely give the nations as Your inheritance, and the very ends of the earth as Your possession. You shall break them with a rod of iron, you shall shatter them like earthenware..." Now therefore, O kings, show discernment... *Worship the Lord with reverence and rejoice with trembling. Do homage to the Son.* (Ps. 2:7-12)

The shepherds made haste to find the babe and to look into the face of the One who shattered all thrones set against Him. He would shake the very foundations of Judea and the uttermost parts of the world. His light would sever the darkness, though the world would not comprehend it. He would distinguish between those who walk in truth and those who do not. He would claim His own and lead a kingdom that would stand forever. He would provide peace between sinful man and a holy God.

There, in the midst of a dark place, stands a Christmas tree. By the looks of its boughs and needles, it has existed before the beginning. Nothing grand about its appearance with its wounded trunk and mended branches. Its symmetry is marred with unruly offshoots that seem to overtake the lush arms and weight it down in places unbecoming. But a star has settled on this one. And on this night a few take notice of its sustaining posture. It is apparent a certain branch, once a shoot but now supporting the rest, crowns this tree with evergreen. We are captivated by its great humility. By that attribute alone, we fear it may be cut down. It will, one day.[3] But we have no doubt it is by *this* Christmas Tree we will live. Our eyes "have seen Your salvation, which You have prepared in the presence of all peoples, a Light of revelation to the Gentiles, and the glory of Your people Israel" (Luke 2:30-32).

> And the Word became flesh, and dwelt among us, and we saw His glory, glory as of the only begotten from the Father, full of grace and truth. (John 1:14)

Joy to the world! The Lord has come!

EXPERIENCE

In the observance of Advent, many people around the world will light the last candle – the Jesus Candle – on Christmas Day. Consider lighting a candle this morning and keeping it lit today to remind you and your family of the gift of our Savior. Every time you see the candle burning brightly, remember that like Adam we once fell under the curse of sin, but He came to crush our accuser. Like Abraham, we were once inhabitants of a pagan land, but He has promised us blessing. Like Moses, we were once in bondage, but He has set us free. Like Rahab, we were once estranged to His family, but He has come to adopt us as His own. Like Boaz, He has come to redeem us and give us hope. Like David, He was looked upon as the least of these, but took the throne to rule in our hearts. Like King Jehoiachin, we were guilty of rebellion, but He came to make us like Zerubbabel, a child of grace.

All praise and glory be to our Savior, the One we celebrate today! He has come and He is coming again!

[Jesus said,] "Behold, I am coming quickly... I am the Alpha and the

3 Heb. 2

Omega, the first and the last, the beginning and the end... I am the root and the descendant of David, the bright morning star... Yes, I am coming quickly." Amen. Come, Lord Jesus. (Rev. 22:12,16,20)

ABOUT THE AUTHOR

Riki Yarbrough lives in Waco, Texas, with her husband and three children. She is an artist, in both graphic design and mixed media, and has taught Bible studies for women at church and in other ministries. A strong sense of adventure propels her and her family in their pursuits. Riki's perspective is bent on process, loving the creative journey almost more than the outcome. Her days are cataloged with these sojourns from artwork to poetry, hiking and baking, studying and building. Currently, Riki is working toward completing a poetic journey through Passover, with complementing artwork, springing from another personal study and family tradition.